KU-781-420

7000222179

University of the West of England BRISTOL		BOLLAND LIBRARY

MEDIUM LOAN COLLECTION
Please ensure that this book is returned by the end of the loan period for which it is issued.

UWE, BRISTOL   7555B.06.04
Printing & Stationery Services

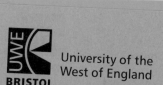

0 3. NOV 2004		21. FEB 2007
1 7. NOV 2004	15. FEB 2005	26. FEB 2007
2 4. NOV 2004	1 6. MAR 2005	✓
	2 3. JUN 2005	1 2. NOV 2007
0 1. DEC 2004	0 2. NOV 2005	10 DEC 2007
	0 9. NOV 2005	
0 8. DEC 2004	1 5. DEC 2005	
	2 0. FEB 2006	2 1. JAN 2008
15. DEC 2004		2 APR 2008
		1 8. APR 2008
1 0. JAN 2005	2 8. FEB 2006	
	0 4. DEC 2006	2 9. MAY 2008
		1 6. FEB 2009

Telephone Renewals: 0117 328 2092 (24 hours)
Library Web Address: www.uwe.ac.uk/library

Counselling & Psychotherapy in Focus

Series Editor: Windy Dryden, Goldsmiths College,
University of London

Counselling & Psychotherapy in Focus is a series of books which
examines the criticisms directed at different forms of counselling
and psychotherapy. Each book in the series reviews the critiques of
a particular approach, presents counter-arguments to the criticisms
and examines the influence that the debates have had in shaping
the approach in question. The books in this series are:

David Livingstone Smith
Psychoanalyses in Focus

Mark Rivett and Eddy Street
Family Therapy in Focus

Paul Wilkins
Person-Centred Therapy in Focus

Person-Centred Therapy in Focus

Paul Wilkins

UWE, BRISTOL

18 JUN 2003

PSY

Library Services

SAGE Publications

London • Thousand Oaks • New Delhi

© Paul Wilkins 2003

First published 2003

Apart from any fair dealing for the purposes of research or
private study, or criticism or review, as permitted under the
Copyright, Designs and Patents Act, 1988, this publication
may be reproduced, stored or transmitted in any form, or by
any means, only with the prior permission in writing of the
publishers, or in the case of reprographic reproduction, in
accordance with the terms of licences issued by the Copyright
Licensing Agency. Inquiries concerning reproduction outside
those terms should be sent to the publishers.

 SAGE Publications Ltd
6 Bonhill Street
London EC2A 4PU

SAGE Publications Inc.
2455 Teller Road
Thousand Oaks, California 91320

SAGE Publications India Pvt Ltd
B-42, Panchsheel Enclave
Post Box 4109
New Delhi 110 017

British Library Cataloguing in Publication data

A catalogue record for this book is available
from the British Library

ISBN 0 7619 6486 X
ISBN 0 7619 6487 8 (pbk)

Library of Congress Control Number: 2002141272

UWE, BRISTOL LIBRARY SERVICES

Typeset by C&M Digitals (P) Ltd., Chennai, India
Printed in Great Britain by TJ International Ltd, Padstow,
Cornwall

Contents

Acknowledgements

My particular thanks go to my friend and colleague Keith Tudor for his critical reading of an early draft of my manuscript and his helpful and constructive comments. My thanks too to Dave Mearns for his encouraging feedback and his helpful suggestions as to how my manuscript could be improved. Jerold Bozarth too deserves a special mention for the way he freely offered his opinions when I asked about thorny matters of theory and practice. They and many others have been instrumental in my thinking.

Author's Note

As with any other approach to counselling and psychotherapy, person-centred counselling has a peculiar language. Its theorists and practitioners make reference to (for example) 'necessary and sufficient conditions', 'the fully functioning person', 'actualising' and 'formative' tendencies, 'conditions of worth', and so on. In this book, I assume a certain familiarity with this language in as much as I do not always define my terms. For those wishing to know more about person-centred theory and practice, there are several accessible but comprehensive introductory texts – perhaps the most notable of these is Mearns and Thorne (1988 or 1999, 2nd edn). There is a shorter account (and therefore necessarily less thorough) in Wilkins (1999). Merry (1995) issues an Invitation to Person-Centred Psychology and in Kirschenbaum and Henderson (1990a) there is an anthology of Rogers' own writing covering a period of 45 years. More recently, Tudor and Merry (2002) have given us a Dictionary of Person-Centred Psychology which provides a comprehensive and cross-referenced work covering all aspects of the person-centred approach.

1
Introduction: So Just What *is* Person-Centred Therapy?

Perhaps it seems strange to start by asking such an obvious question as 'What is person-centred therapy?' yet the more I think about the criticisms of the person-centred approach I commonly hear, the more it seems that many of them are rooted in misunderstandings and ignorance. For example, there appears to be a belief that being 'person-centred' involves somehow being 'nice' to people, listening to them with a sympathetic ear but doing little else. It is quite common for therapists of other orientations to say that this may be helpful in the initial stages of a therapeutic relationship (if indeed it is helpful at all) but that the serious work happens when there is a switch to some other modality.

More charitably (or perhaps indulgently – even paternalistically), it is allowed that person-centred therapy 'works' for the 'worried well' but anyone who is more seriously disturbed, 'mentally ill', in some way limited as to the 'depth' to which they can proceed or has 'deep-rooted' problems, 'needs' the stronger medicine of another approach. This is exemplified by the view of Kovel (1976: 116) who writes: 'Rogerian treatment works best where the person doesn't have to go very deep – as with the student needing to steady down – or where, practically speaking, he can't – as with chronic schizophrenics in a hospital.'

Quite why this view of person-centred therapy persists in the face of what looks to practitioners of the approach to be convincing evidence to the contrary is at first difficult to understand. But perhaps there are explanations? For example, Mearns and Thorne (2000: ix–x) who are puzzled by the widespread misunderstanding of person-centred theory and practice attribute this to the threat these are to therapists of other orientations. They write:

[W]e ... are baffled by the misconceptions which still abound about the theory and practice of person-centred therapy. We ask ourselves how it can be, for example, that despite the growing and impressive body of literature about the approach, despite the almost universal respect in which its originator, Carl Rogers, is held, despite the existence of countless person-centred therapists and their clients, there still exists the denigratory and scurrilous myth that person-centred therapists merely nod, reflect the last words of their client and can only be trusted with the most superficial concerns of middle-class clients. We have concluded that such misconceptions are not always the outcome of ignorance but in some cases, at least, have much deeper roots. It would seem that our approach has the strange capacity to threaten practitioners from other orientations so that they seek refuge in wilful ignorance or in condemnatory dismissiveness.

These strong words are echoed by my own experience and belief for how else can the impressive body of theory and the many accounts of practice (as evidenced in this book) be apparently so overlooked for so long? But perhaps we person-centred therapists bear some responsibility? Have we hidden our light under a bushel? This sense that perhaps we have preached principally to the converted seems to be behind the decision of some person-centred writers (for example, Mearns 1999; Tudor 2000; and, in a smaller way, Wilkins 1997a) to publish in widely read professional journals rather than the exclusively person-centred press or even the 'more prestigious' academic journals. The objective is to reach as wide a readership as possible. Has our resistance to conventional hierarchical organisa-tion done us and our clients few favours? The experience of person-centred therapists who attended the First World Congress for Psychotherapy in Vienna in 1996 was that the approach was easily dismissed because we were not represented by a properly consti-tuted professional body. This contributed to the efforts to organise both internationally and in Europe and thence to the formation of the World Association for Person-Centered and Experiential Psychotherapy and Counseling. These questions too are considered implicitly and explicitly in this text.

The view of person-centred therapy as relatively trivial leads some therapists to the belief that they must add something to it to be effec-tive and so to making what to me are extraordinary (even impossi-ble) claims about their orientation, such as 'I am person-centred/psychodynamic.' This implies belief in two contradictory models of the person, two radically different ways of thinking about people and how they function and possibly does profound disservice to both. Merry (1990: 17) puts it thus:

> I am troubled by two things. One is the way the term 'person-centred' is becoming widely used to describe situations which do not do justice to the spirit or the original meaning of that term – 'person-centred hypnotherapy', for example. The other ... is the growing, but mistaken

view, that client-centred therapy has no distinct or unique identity, but is simply a means of providing a psychological climate in which other techniques, methods and approaches can be applied.

Maybe too the fact that many counsellor training courses in the UK are influenced by the ideas and practices underlying person-centred therapy has contributed to these misunderstandings. Hutterer (1993: 279) expresses a concern widespread in the person-centred community:

> The same adage might apply to person-centred therapy which was once used about the English language: the English language is so much liked and so widely used as an international business language and conference language because it can so quickly be spoken so poorly.
> In a similar way one suspects that client-centred therapy is often taught primarily, and wrongly, because it is believed to be easy to learn. In fact the idea seems to be that everyone can learn it: it just takes some friendly and understanding person. There are probably in no other therapy form so many who think so soon that they have already mastered it, even without training.

Actually, there is a big difference between being trained as a person-centred therapist and acquiring a set of skills which draw (sometimes very loosely) on the thought and practices of Carl Rogers. The former requires a great deal more theoretical knowledge than a passing acquaintance with the so-called core conditions. Also it means acquiring a thorough grounding in the practicalities of relating to clients, attention to the self-development of the practitioner, probably including extensive experience in a peer group and many hours of supervised practice. The easiest (but not the only) way to acquire these skills and experiences is to attend a training course acknowledged as person-centred by the person-centred community. A course which has person-centred counselling as a core model, even if accredited by the BACP (British Association for Counselling and Psychotherapy), does not necessarily offer a full training in person-centred therapy. Mearns (1997) writes extensively on person-centred counselling training and (p. x) points out that:

> the need to explore the requirements for person-centred training is emphasised by the fact that person-centred counselling is extremely dangerous for practitioners who have insufficient training ....
> Person-centred counselling probably requires more training and a greater intensity of training than most other mainstream counselling approaches because of the daunting personal development objectives which require to be met.

Mearns and Thorne (2000: 25–9) also deal with some of the complexities of training effective person-centred therapists. It is clear that, to be adequately trained in person-centred therapy, practitioners need not only to understand the body of person-centred theory – which goes far beyond a knowledge of the conditions of congruence, empathic understanding and unconditional positive regard – but also to have paid considerable attention to personal development. This is because, as important as a sound grasp of theory is, personal growth is equally important because the therapist's self is central to the therapeutic endeavour.

The teaching of 'person-centred' skills on relatively short courses appears to have led to a lot of well-meant 'mislabelling' on the part of some practising counsellors who may think that they have been trained in person-centred practice but who, from my perspective, have a limited idea of what this means. Mearns (1997: 192) writes about the traditional weakness of person-centred training courses with respect to the teaching of theory. He echoes my fears (and those of many other person-centred practitioners), writing:

> Perhaps the worst consequences of this state of affairs was that the person-centred approach became an easy target for those who wanted to attach themselves to an approach which felt intrinsically attractive but which did not make excessive learning demands upon them. I am astonished at the number of people I meet who call themselves 'person-centred counsellors' who have undertaken little or no training and certainly not an intensive Diploma level course.

I suspect this may be behind the (unsubstantiated and quite possibly apocryphal) assertion that more BACP members who describe themselves as 'person-centred' are complained of than members of any other orientation. Of course this may be because there are more 'person-centred' counsellors than any other kind but I wonder if a lack of clarity about theory and practice is also a factor? Mearns and Thorne (1988: 2) expressed their 'horror' at this situation. They wrote:

> We are little short of horrified by the recent proliferation of counselling practitioners, both in America and Britain, who seem to believe that by sticking the label 'person-centred' on themselves they have licence to follow the most bizarre promptings of their own intuition or to create a veritable smorgasbord of therapeutic approaches which smack of eclecticism at its most irresponsible.

Of course, even well-trained practitioners thoroughly conversant with the principles of person-centred therapy are as capable of unprofessional or unethical behaviour as therapists of any other orientation – but that is just my point – *as* likely, not more or less likely.

The Person-Centred Approach, Client-Centred Therapy and Person-Centred Counselling

As within many other orientations, there is within the person-centred tradition a plethora of terms which are possible sources of confusion. In the first place, there is what may be viewed as an 'umbrella' term, the person-centred *approach*. This is sometimes used (somewhat imprecisely) to refer to the various ways of practising counselling and psychotherapy which draw principally on the work of Carl Rogers and his successors. But it is much more than this. Wood (1996: 163) points out that:

> The person-centered approach is not a psychology, a psychotherapy, a philosophy, a school, a movement or many other things frequently imagined. It is merely what its name suggests, an *approach*. It is a psychological posture, a way of being, from which one confronts a situation.

This 'way of being' (p. 169) has the following elements:

- a belief in a formative directional tendency
- a will to help
- an intention to be effective in one's objectives
- compassion for the individual and respect for his or her autonomy and dignity
- a flexibility in thought and action
- an openness to new discoveries
- 'an ability to intensely concentrate and clearly grasp the linear, piece by piece, appearance of reality as well as perceiving it holistically or all-at-once'
- a tolerance for uncertainty or ambiguity

Wood (p. 174) considers that:

> Applying the person-centered approach ... means confronting a phenomenon (such as psychotherapy, classroom learning, encounter groups or large groups) with that certain way of being ... which may also include not only respecting others, but being able to deal with hostility and skepticism. It may mean facing both the unknown and one's own fears and doubt. It may mean fighting for one's own ideas, but giving them up for better ones. It frequently requires an active patience: to allow various perspectives to become apparent before deciding, while, at the same time, not withholding one's vital participation while data is accumulating.

I am not sure that I fully accept Wood's distinction between an 'approach' and a philosophy. At least in lay person's terms, anything

\y of being' that is a particular way of encountering
: to a philosophy. The person-centred approach is
'in effect, a way of being in relationship. This
ith the self, another individual, a group or even a
ᴜe applied to many areas of human interaction.' The
...ᴄᴎ may be applied not only to counselling and psychotherapy
ᴜut to many other areas of human endeavour, for example education
(see, for example, Rogers 1983), interpersonal relationships (see, for
example, Rogers 1970), political, cultural and social change (see,
for example, Rogers 1977, 1980) and research (see, for example,
Mearns and McLeod 1984) but perhaps most famously to counselling
and psychotherapy (between which person-centred practitioners make
no distinction). The important elements of the approach as I see them
are the drive for 'growth' (that is the formative and actualising tendencies) and the consideration of individuals as inherently trustworthy
(which has implications for the exercise of power). The person-centred
approach to therapy focuses first and foremost on the relationship
between counsellor and client. Mearns (1996: 306) points out that, in
his very first book, Rogers used the term 'relationship therapy' to
describe his approach to work with clients. By the time the classic text
of person-centred therapy was published (see Rogers 1951), the term
'client-centred' was preferred because, in the words of Thorne (1991:
27), it 'put the emphasis on the internal world of the client and focused
attention on the attitudes of therapists towards their clients rather than
on particular techniques'. The epithet 'person-centred' is of later origin
and Mearns and Thorne (1988: 1–2) explain the rationale underlying
its adoption. As well as pointing out its broader meaning, they write:

> It seems to us that the counselling relationships in which we engage
> require of us the utmost concentration on, and awareness of, our
> own thoughts, feelings, sensations and intuitions in the moment-to-
> moment interaction with our clients. If the truth be known we are not
> merely focused on the world of our clients. We are concerned to be in
> touch with ourselves as much as with them, and to monitor cease-
> lessly the relationship between us. Person-centred counselling there-
> fore seems a thoroughly apt description of our work, for we are at all
> times in this highly concentrated way committed as persons to other
> persons who seek our help.

In a later work, Mearns and Thorne (2000: 15) restate their beliefs
as person-centred therapists thus:

> Essentially we continue to have confidence in the resourcefulness of
> the human being and in his or her ability to lead a constructive,

positive, life-affirming and socially creative existence. We believe that human beings flourish best when they can experience acceptance and understanding rather than adverse judgement and a lack of responsiveness from others. We are profoundly committed to offering ourselves to our clients without simulation and to moving into relational depth with them when they invite and welcome us there.

This neatly synthesises the person-centred theories of the model of the person and constructive personality change and the essentials of the practice of person-centred therapy. Sanders (2000: 67) also offers an elegant statement of the principles of person-centred therapy. These he divides into 'primary' and 'secondary' principles which (slightly adapted) are:

Primary Principles

- The primacy of the actualising tendency – it is a therapeutic mistake to believe, or act upon the belief, that the therapeutic change process is *not* motivated by the client's actualising tendency.
- Assertion of the necessity of the conditions for therapeutic change set out in Rogers (1957) – it is a therapeutic mistake to *exclude* any of the conditions. *Passive* inclusion, assuming that such conditions are always present in all relationships is also insufficient. This principle requires active attention to the provision of these conditions.
- Primacy of the non-directive attitude *at least* at the level of content but not necessarily at the level of process. It is permissible for the therapist to be an expert process-director – it is a therapeutic mistake to direct the content of a client's experience either explicitly or implicitly.

Secondary Principles

- Autonomy and the client's right to self-determination – it is a therapeutic mistake to violate the client's internal locus of control.
- Equality, or the non-expertness of the therapist – it is a therapeutic mistake to imply that the therapist is an expert in the direction of the content and substance of the client's life.
- The primacy of the non-directive attitude and intention in its absolute and pure form – it is a therapeutic mistake to wrest control of the change process from the client's actualising tendency in any way whatsoever.
- The sufficiency of the conditions for therapeutic change set out in Rogers (1957) – it is a therapeutic mistake to *include* other methods.
- Holism – it is a therapeutic mistake to respond to only part of the organism.

The term client-centred counselling/therapy or even 'classic' client-centred counselling/therapy (see Sanders 2000: 69) is increasingly reserved for an approach which adheres to the principles set out by Rogers in his publications of 1951, 1957 and 1959 and *only* those – that is which operates in a way which is in accord with both Sanders' primary *and* secondary principles. 'Person-centred counselling/ therapy' may be understood to be an umbrella term embracing approaches which, although derived from the same key principles, allow some operational differences with respect to the secondary principles and for some flexibility with respect to theory. Sanders (2000: 68) writes:

> In order to be in the 'family' of therapies identified as 'person-centred', theory and practice must be based on all of the primary principles. They are necessary. Secondary principles can be held as the basis for theory and practice as desired.

At first, this may seem to be at odds with the statement of Rogers (1987: 13) 'whether I am called upon for help in a relationship deemed to be client-centered or one that is labelled person-centered I work the same way in each' and the stated belief of Bozarth (1998: 24) that the terms 'person-centered' and 'client-centered' are essentially the same, but I think Sanders is making a useful distinction which would be acceptable to each. In this book, my use of the term 'person-centred therapy' is in accordance with the description of Mearns and Thorne and the definition of Sanders. It is questions about the theories and practices of this 'family' which I address, not those of the bizarre, irresponsible eclectics who Mearns and Thorne indicate attribute to themselves the label 'person-centred'. In a way, I am seeking to evaluate person-centred therapy according to the terms in which its practitioners define it rather than those imposed upon it from outside.

One Nation but Many Tribes?

Sanders' (2000) helpful scheme for understanding who is and who is not covered by the umbrella of the person-centred approach implies that there is more than one way of being a person-centred therapist. This variety had been previously explored by Margaret Warner who asks whether the person-centred approach is one nation with many tribes. Warner (1998, reproduced in the ADPCA Reader 1999) explores the tension in the attitudes of those who claim to espouse the person-centred approach. She (p. 3) writes:

> Therapists disagree passionately as to what is really 'client-centered' or 'person-centered' and whether the two are the same. Some would

include almost all therapies that have some emphasis on genuineness or empathy as client-centered. Others would define the term client-centered therapy very narrowly, in ways that would limit its application to a much smaller group of practitioners – those who follow the radically nondirective elements evident in taped versions of Rogers' psychotherapy practice.

Warner (pp. 5–6) goes on to explore the arguments of a variety of therapists describing themselves as person-centred before reaching the conclusion, 'the differences among these positions are substantial'. She (pp. 6–8) characterises psychotherapy as divided according to five 'levels of interventiveness'. These are:

Level 1: *The therapist is in contact with the client without bringing anything from outside the client's frame of reference.* This she regards as 'a largely hypothetical category'.

Level 2: *The therapist uses personal experiences and theories as a way to more fully understand the client's frame of reference, without trying to influence or alter the client's experience.* This she describes as an attempt 'to walk in the client's shoes'. This is the position of classic client-centred therapists.

Level 3: *The therapist brings material into the therapeutic relationship in ways that foster the client's choice as to whether and how to use such material.* The therapist may bring suggestions or interpretations, etc., to the encounter but the client is free to make use of or disregard them. I see much of person-centred approaches to creative and expressive therapies as rooted here. Many would also place experiential psychotherapy in this category.

Level 4: *The therapist brings material to the therapy relationship from his or her frame of reference from a position of authority or expertise.* Here, the therapist is clearly 'leading' the client.

Level 5: *The therapist brings material that is outside the client's frame of reference in such a way that the client is unaware of interventions and/or the therapist's actual purposes in introducing the interventions.* Here an element of deception (for example paradoxical instructions) may be used.

Warner believes there to be a major disjunction between levels 3 and 4 and that practitioners operating on levels 1, 2 or 3 may legitimately adopt the label 'person-centred'. I find Warner's ideas helpful; they explain why I can call myself a person-centred psycho-dramatist (a level 3 mode of operation) but I also wonder if more is obscured than revealed? For me (and others) this is typified by the unresolved debate about the use of techniques (see Wilkins 1994a, 2000b and Chapter 7).

Taken together, Warner (1998/1999) and Sanders (2000) offer a theoretical framework in which a continuum of approaches to psychotherapy characterised by a belief in the actualising tendency can be understood as 'person-centred'. This continuum corresponds to a 'directivity' dimension with the classic client-centred position described by Sanders (and characterised by, for example, the work and ideas of Barbara Brodley) at one end and the process-experiential position (growing from 'focusing' as described by Gendlin 1978, and characterised by, for example, the thought of Germain Lietaer) at the other. Rennie (1998: 5) seems to propose an extension to the continuum offering the thought that, in some respects at least, process-experiential therapists occupy a middle ground 'between the literal Rogerians and Gendlians', by which he means classic client-centred therapists and those for whom focusing is the main approach to therapy. Rennie considers himself to occupy this middle ground and his book is entitled *Person-Centred Counselling: An Experiential Approach* (Rennie 1998). In adopting this title, he is identifying both his nation (person-centred) and his tribe (experiential).

There is a recognition that there are two major but related approaches to psychotherapy in the person-centred 'family' in the increasingly common tendency to 'jointly label' our organisations as person-(or client-)centred *and* experiential. Thus one of our major international gatherings has been known as the International Conference for Client-Centered and Experiential Psychotherapy, and our new association is the World Association for Person-Centered and Experiential Psychotherapy and Counseling. Of course, as is implicit in the notion of one nation but many tribes, the picture is really much more complicated in that, even along the directivity continuum, there is more than one underpinning theory – for example Natalie Rogers' person-centred expressive therapy might be seen by some as just as 'directive' as Rennie's (1998) experiential approach but they do not necessarily agree in their models of the person and ideas about how a therapist acts. Also, there are disagreements as to (at the more directive end) who can legitimately call themselves person-centred and there are certainly limits to person-centred therapy which are not just to do with 'directivity' but also (and for example) attitudes taken to the agents of change and the role of the unconscious. For me, well within the boundaries of person-centred therapy (that is clearly in accord with Warner's levels 1, 2 or 3 and at least Sanders' 'essential' criteria) are not only the experiential approaches but (for example) also those with a creative/expressive dimension (including person-centred expressive therapy, person-centred art therapy and person-centred psychodrama), person-centred play therapy (see Barrett-Lennard 1998: 123–30) and the 'family therapy' of Gaylin (see Gaylin 2001). In addition, person-centred theory extends beyond both classic client-centred and experiential dimensions to embrace (among the work of many others as this book will show) the philosophical insights of Peter Schmid (see Schmid 1996, 1998, 2001a, 2001b) and Ivan Ellingham (see Ellingham 1997, 1999); the thoughtful accounts of Barrett-Lennard (for example, Barrett-Lennard 1998) which often draw extensively on research; and the spiritual dimensions of Thorne (1996), Purton (1998) and Morotomi (1998), to name but a few. So, the person-centred approach to psychotherapy is a broad church and it is for each of us to find our own place in it. Its major wings, nevertheless, are classic client-centred therapy and experiential therapy.

Because, as Pete Sanders in his foreword to *Process Work in Person-Centred Therapy: Phenomenological and Existential Perspectives* (see Worsley 2002: xii) points out, 'experiential psychotherapy and process work will be unfamiliar territory' to many in the UK although 'in mainland Europe experiential psychotherapy and person-centred therapy are seen as practically indivisible', and because I draw on the person-centred tradition as a whole in my responses to the criticisms made of it, a brief explanation of how experiential psychotherapists operate may be helpful.

'Experiential' Responding: Doing it Differently?

Experiential psychotherapy is that branch of person-centred therapy which emanates from the pioneering work of Gendlin (1978) and of which 'focusing' is an integral and essential process. Experiential therapists are more likely than classic client-centred therapists to see responses other than the checking of empathic understanding as appropriate or even necessary to a successful therapeutic endeavour. For example, Lietaer (1993: 32), who considers that sometime around 1960 'client-centred therapy evolved from "non-directive" to "experiential", and this allowed the therapist to bring something from his own frame of reference', sees the expression of personal feelings 'as having *positive potential* [original emphasis] for deepening the therapeutic process'. Therapists who practise in the classic manner or close to it take a different view as to the evolution of person-centred therapy. Bozarth (1998: 78), for example, voices his disagreement with Lietaer's assertion and gives his reasons. Bozarth ends his contradiction of Lietaer's views with the statement:

> [Gendlin's Experiential Therapy is] theoretically related to Rogers' theory but [is] ultimately a deviation from the basic premise of client-centered therapy. The intention of the therapist to direct clients to experiencing violates Rogerian theory by not holding to the strongest degree of self-authority and self-determination of clients.

There are many such disagreements between those who consider themselves 'client-centred' and those who consider themselves 'experiential' – sometimes these disagreements seeming very much like those which occur in any family. Make of that what you will!

Although experiential therapists see themselves as rooted in the client-centred approach as described by Rogers, they have diverged from it, or added to it (depending on your point of view). Experiential therapists do respond empathically; unconditional positive regard and congruence are important to them, but they also see themselves as having the tasks of encouraging their clients to 'focus' and drawing the attention of clients to 'process'. Tudor and Merry (2002: 57) offer the following definition of focusing:

> The process of focusing involves attention to felt but non-verbal sensations leading to more easily recognised and, therefore, more easily verbalised feelings and sensations; new insights and meanings may then follow, with feelings becoming more clearly differentiated and understood; over time, feelings and sensations which originally were only vaguely experienced evolve until they are more fully experienced, and their implications for other aspects of the client's life begin to become apparent.

Leijssen (1998: 133) in her account of focusing discusses the link between stages in the focusing process and person-centred attitudes. She considers that 'facilitating focusing can stay very close to the kind of interactions "good" person-centred practitioners have always offered'. 'Staying close to' is clearly not the same as 'conforming to'. Although experiential therapists are as different from one another in their style as any others, it seems that they are more likely to 'lead' their clients than are classic client-centred therapists. They may draw attention to non-verbal behaviour and (from my perspective) interpret it, challenge, reassure, name feelings the client is (for some reason) reluctant to own and so on. Each of these is likely to be more directive than would normally be acceptable in classic client-centred practice. Leijssen (1998: 144) describes how she might work with a client (Louis):

Client: 'Oh, my life is fine.' The client's angry, nervous gaze and the stamping of his foot don't escape the therapist: 'You're telling me your life is fine, but when I see your body expression I imagine there might be some anger? ... [original ellipsis]. It is OK to feel anger, you may well have good reason.' ... The therapist also names some more of Louis's unmentionable feelings, such as his sadness, his loneliness and his shame. Gradually Louis learns that he can differentiate between various 'annoying' feelings.

There is an element of leadership and an emphasis on modelling by the therapist and the 'learning' of the client here which (among other things) distinguishes experiential psychotherapy from classic client-centred therapy. Rennie (1998) gives an account of the variety of response to a client which may be made by an experiential therapist. As well as (pp. 32–43) 'basic attending skills' which include (p. 38) reflection, Rennie also describes (pp. 44–59) the use of 'vivid language' (that is the visual imagery and metaphors the therapist has in response to the client's material) (pp. 60–70); 'transparency in the relationship' (that is (p. 70), 'the disclosure to the client of how we are experiencing ourselves in relation with the client and/or of how we are experiencing the client'); and (pp. 71–88) 'process identification and process direction' (that is, as well as empathic responding, drawing the attention of clients to their processing of experience either in the present or the past or directing their process). It is perhaps in 'process direction' that experiential therapists move furthest from the original client-centred ideas. Rennie (1998: 81) is unequivocal about the directive and 'expert' qualities needed by the experiential therapist. He states:

When process directing, counsellors take charge. They assume the role of expert – an expert on process. In keeping with the experiential therapies, in this approach to person-centred counselling it is held that there are times when clients need help in dealing with themselves.

It is clear that in their form of person-centred therapy experiential therapists have added to the repertoire of therapist responses but it should be emphasised that for some client-centred therapists the emphasis on experiencing as a cause of therapeutic movement rather than a result of it and the move away from the non-directive attitude means that experiential therapy cannot be considered 'person-centred'. For example, Prouty (1999: 4–11) considers there to be a 'dissonance' between the thought and practice of Carl Rogers and the experiential position.

Questioning the Precepts

When considering classic client-centred or experiential positions from some other perspectives (often from many other perspectives), the ideas and beliefs which underpin the person-centred approach can be questioned and alternatives proposed. These other perspectives are in themselves questionable. None of this really matters except that the believer is aware that belief is a matter of choice – underlying all human thought is an unreasonable proposition, for example, time began (or it did not), there is a Supreme Being (or there is not), and so on. Often, what appears to be 'logical' follows only from the assumption of an unknowable proposition. This assumption may be based on 'evidence' but it is not proven. For example, arguments about human goodness may stem from the attitude taken to the existence and nature of the Supreme Being. By definition, people legitimately adopting the label 'person-centred' have *chosen* to believe in the actualising tendency with its various implications. It is a choice based perhaps on instinct or intuition, perhaps on empirical observation – or all of these and more – but it is a choice and (although there may be 'evidence') not, I think, susceptible to proof. But the same is true of the adoption of any other approach to therapy. Feltham (1999: 1–3) has pointed out that psychotherapy is a 'deeply controversial field' and that therapists tend to adopt a particular position with greater reference to their deeply held beliefs than to demonstrable 'facts'. To choose the person-centred approach does not necessarily mean uncritically accepting the word of Carl Rogers (perhaps because to do so would contradict the very principles he set forward!) nor does it mean that person-centred theory is ossified, stuck somewhere in the mid-to-late twentieth century. In this, I take a different view from Cain (1993: 134) who considers that 'client-centred' therapy

> has changed very little since its inception. There are numerous factors that have contributed to its stagnation and declining influence. One important factor is the enormous and continuing influence of Rogers' ideas and therapeutic style on those who model themselves after him and encourage their students and colleagues to do so.

Cain is apparently unaware of the developments made (and still being made) in Europe, Japan and increasingly Latin America, Southern Africa and Australia. Here the approach is certainly not stagnant and is arguably gaining in influence. However, what he says about the taking of the thought and practices of Rogers as having developed into almost sacred principles is worth noting. I know that

I should also say that I do not see the person-centred approach as all-encompassing – but I think I probably do, even though I know this is irrational and that, paradoxically, I do not see other belief systems as invalid.

Of course, the person-centred discourse is susceptible to criticism. Some of these criticisms stem from criticisms of psychotherapy *per se* (although its proponents tend to see person-centred therapy as rooted in a critique of 'psychotherapy', that is, as a reaction to psychoanalytic and cognitive-behavioural theories and practices), and some come from within the psychotherapy discourse. What follows in Chapters 3 to 10 is an examination of some of the most frequently encountered criticisms of person-centred therapy and my answers to them, but in order to appreciate person-centred therapy fully it is helpful to understand something of its contexts and the political and social beliefs which are commonly held to underpin it. These, too, are susceptible to criticism.

2
'More than Just a Psychotherapy': An Important Social and Political Context or Unjustified Complacency?

There is within the person-centred approach to counselling and psychotherapy a tendency to think of our theory and practice as being all-encompassing – that is, that the necessary and sufficient conditions and a belief in the actualising tendency are all that is needed to address all human ills, all ways of being. Moreover, there is a widespread tendency to see person-centred values, when appropriately applied, as adequate to bring about social and political change. Although they are in some ways peripheral to the notion of person-centred therapy, these other dimensions of the approach do pertain and, because they constitute part of the philosophical framework in which therapeutic practice takes place, they are worthy of consideration. To entirely separate person-centred therapy from the context of the person-centred approach means that any consideration of it is incomplete. What follows is an examination of some of the attitudes and political and social ideas likely to underpin the practice of person-centred therapy and some of the challenges to these principles.

Encompassing 'Difference': Liberal/Humanist Oppression?

The feminist movement has encouraged an exploration of the experiences of men and women and led to a more widespread acknowledgement that these are different. Men and women are different not only in terms of biology and the daily experience of power and oppression, but also in terms of psychological development. Although this difference of development is unacknowledged in Rogers' models, it has been considered by later person-centred theorists. Wolter-Gustafson (1999: 119–214), for example, skilfully examines Rogers' theory of human development with reference to (among others) feminist and postmodern understandings and (p. 212) finds 'several potential areas for collaboration and theoretical alignment'. In her view, this collaboration between person-centred thinkers and a variety of others could lead to a 'more fully functioning paradigm of research, study and practice that truly honors all human beings'. Writing more personally, Natiello (1999: 163–71) shows how conditions of worth lead to gender splitting and how these may be healed through the person-centred approach. She also considers the challenges that gender typing brings to the congruence of women and the different challenges to the congruence of men. For example, women learn to suppress their anger, men are not supposed to be caring and gentle. So, it seems that in the experience of some women, the person-centred approach is an effective way of working with differences arising from gender and that this can be placed in the framework of person-centred theory.

Warner (1999: 193–8) argues that the very language of psychology (she includes psychotherapy) may be oppressive because it allows the psychologist to define the experience of the other. She is particularly concerned with the experience of women and writes (p. 197): 'Women have a long history of having others define their realities for them in various covert ways', but clearly believes this statement applies to the experience of any less powerful group. She states (p. 193):

Typically within society, those in higher positions of authority define the reality of those in lesser positions. The rich define the reality of the poor, men define the reality of women, adults define the reality of children, English Americans define the reality of other American ethnic groups.

In the field of psychology, she sees the use of 'compacted language', in which 'psychological phenomena are described as if they were objects with stable qualities rather than human experiences', as contributing to this oppression. Although she does not say so, Warner clearly believes the language of the 'process expert' (a description adopted by some person-centred practitioners) which is descriptive and action-oriented is to be preferred. She adds: 'We should expect psychologists to communicate with clients in ways that acknowledge that they have legitimate, separate personal and cultural realities' (p. 197). With its avoidance of interpretation, diagnosis and technical language, the person-centred approach goes at least some way to meeting Warner's criteria. But is this enough?

Wheeler (in Wheeler and McLeod 1995: 286–7) expresses her admiration for the 'anti-intellectual, non-racist, non-sexist' qualities inherent in the person-centred approach, and certainly the high value person-centred practitioners place on unconditional positive regard means we like to see ourselves as minimally judgemental. But in some analyses liberal humanism (a term which may legitimately be used to describe person-centred values) is itself oppressive. When I am challenged with the assertion that my way of being, which I see as open and accepting, valuing people for themselves rather than for their ethnicity, sexuality or religion, is in fact oppressive, I have no easy answer. If what I value is subjective experience and (for example) a gay man experiences my stance, my value system, as oppressive, then – uncomfortable as this is – I have to accept it. As the result of her research, Galgut (1999: 92) wonders if the very nature of the person-centred relationship could, 'at least in some ways, be unintentionally oppressive and silencing of the lesbian client rather than facilitative?' She explains how the person-centred counsellor's normal way of being in relationship might in effect silence a lesbian woman (and by inference anybody else with a way of being which is 'different', who is marginalised, or who belongs to a minority group). Addressing the (presumed) heterosexual counsellor, she writes:

> You and I are, in the first instance at any rate, just a microcosm of that society, in which you wield the power, whether you want to or not, because I don't know where you stand in relation to me as a lesbian. I will assume you are heterosexual, unless I already know otherwise or you tell me differently, and I'll worry about your attitude towards me. I need you to accept what I consider your responsibility here and make it safe enough for me to disclose my sexuality. (1999: 93)

Galgut goes on to point out that her study may be seen to refute the cherished person-centred notion that the demonstration of the necessary and sufficient conditions will make it obvious to the lesbian client that her sexuality is acceptable to the therapist. Somehow the disinclination of person-centred therapists to ask questions from their own frames of reference for fear of deflecting clients from their own flow of experiencing becomes oppressive. If Galgut is right (and she obviously writes from her own experience and this must be given credence), then the 'non-directivity' of person-centred practice is having exactly the opposite effect of what is intended. Of course, it could be argued that a sufficiently empathic practitioner would pick up on the lesbian client's difficulty and in some way respond to it – this might facilitate the desired safety and consequent disclosure, but what about all those times when this empathic sensing is not there? Galgut suggests that every client be offered the opportunity to disclose but is 'not exactly sure how to facilitate this' (p. 93). Her conclusion is that, at an early stage, it would be helpful if the client is told something positive about the therapist and this is followed with a statement of non-discrimination.

This story of the consequences of the practitioner's failure to raise the issue of difference I seem to have heard many times – about race and religion as well as sexuality. The argument seems to be that it is the experience of people from minority groups their difference is (perhaps especially in liberal humanist terms) taboo. Not speaking of the difference, but proceeding on the bland (and manifestly untrue) assumption that 'we are all equal' amounts to a denial of their essential selves. It is up to the person with the power (in the context of the society to which I belong, typically a white, heterosexual, middle-class person – I have omitted 'male' because in many ways we are a minority in the world of therapy) to ask, to notice or whatever. Not to do so perpetuates the power imbalance which is the daily experience of someone who is 'different'.

It seems to me that the person-centred approach does have a case to answer here. Like Galgut, I do not know what this answer may be. I am reluctant to start every relationship with a list of questions about sexuality, ethnicity, religious belief and 'aberrant' behaviour for this would seem to lead me away from being 'client-centred', but at the same time I know that people I have encountered have suffered because the difference they felt so deeply was not picked up on and responded to. For example, I worked with a young woman who looked like the other young women in the group, had an English name and spoke with a local accent but who felt set apart because she was born of a Turkish mother and spent her early years in Turkey. From her perspective, she was an alien in a strange land – and nobody noticed! Well, it did come out, arguably because she had learnt to trust the acceptance she was offered by me and the rest of the group – but it came out much later and perhaps in a more desperate way than was necessary. But I have the contrary experience too. Working with a black client and being aware that it was thought by some that the issue of race should, at an early opportunity, be raised by the white therapist, I did bring up the subject at an early stage. This seemed counter-productive and to deflect her. Perhaps I had been awkward and clumsy but certainly my attempt to address our 'inequality' was not well received.

As far as I know, this whole area of working with people who are culturally different is under-explored in terms of person-centred theory and practice (indeed, that is the assertion made in Holdstock 1990, 1993 among others). There is a widespread assumption that the attitudinal conditions are 'good enough' in any relationship. Also, there are (for example) black and gay person-centred practitioners whose thought and practice seems to be in the mainstream of the approach – I think this is probably taken as evidence that the person-centred approach is generally applicable without modification. Rogers appears to take the view that there are universal human qualities which override cultural differences. He writes:

> One of the most striking things about international groups is that they are so similar to every other encounter group. The national and racial and cultural differences come to seem unimportant as the *person* is discovered. In spite of all the differences, there is a great potential for understanding and closeness in the human issues we are all trying to cope with. (Kirschenbaum and Henderson 1990a: 444)

On a personal level, this is my experience of being in multi-cultural groups – but it is also true that 'difference' has been a feature of these groups and this has served as a focus for pain and distress. I am not sure how well I have truly understood my gay, black or Jewish colleagues. I suppose that for a 'perfect' person-centred practitioner, one who was empathic, accepting and congruent under any conditions, in any relationship, difference would not be a problem. But I know of no one like that. It seems to me that we (the white, heterosexual majority) have to find a way of acknowledging (for example) the gay, lesbian and black experiences and that our attempts at conveying unconditional positive regard (which may work well enough with people who experience themselves as culturally equivalent) at least sometimes fall short of the mark. Following on from this acknowledgement is the need to address the shortfall. How? I do not yet know but it may be that 'culture' is the important area here. Singh and Tudor (1997: 32–46) present an analysis of 'cultural conditions for therapy', offering (p. 36) 'a middle ground between cultural compatibility and universalism' – that is, between the notion that client and therapist must be 'crudely' matched according to gross cultural variables ('race, gender, sexuality or disability alone') and the idea that, because human nature has universal qualities, therapeutic skills are universally transferable. They argue that consideration should be given to a range of cultural variables (p. 35). These are:

- **Ethnographic variables** – including nationality, ethnicity, language and religion (or religious tradition).
- **Demographic variables** – including age, gender and place of residence.
- **Status variables** – including those which are social (e.g. class), economic (e.g. nature of employment), educational and political.

The Person-Centred Approach: Agent for Social Change or the New Opiate of the Masses?

A challenge, perhaps to psychotherapy in general and certainly to what is seen to be the person-centred emphasis on the importance of the 'person', is the criticism that attention is directed away from the need for social change, and responsibility is thrown back on the individual. Moreover, therapy directs energy towards inward change and although 'feelings' may be different, 'real' situations remain oppressive, depressive or repressive. There is little point in helping people change if they are then compelled to live in the systems which distressed them in the first place – it is not personal change which is desirable but political change. This argument is made from Marxist and feminist perspectives, among others. For example, Waterhouse (1993: 68) in her feminist critique of person-centred therapy writes: 'in failing to politicize personal life, the Rogerian tradition can be naive and even, at times, harmful'. There is some suggestion that this applies less to the person-centred approach (and to gestalt therapy, co-counselling, and most especially to feminist therapy) than it does to other approaches to therapy. For example, Rowan and Dryden (1988: 7) record that the person-centred approach has 'historically been associated with radical groups and political awareness'. Tudor (1997: 4–10) provides a thoughtful contribution to 'developing a *person-centred approach* to understanding the political nature of the personal and, particularly, the personal nature of the political'. He develops a person-centred analysis of the political sphere with reference to the British general election of 1997, the devolution of power in Scotland and Wales, and the death of Diana, Princess of Wales. Hannon (2001: 4–17) proposes an integration of critical theory and the person-centred approach which he sees as a basis for working towards social transformation. He writes (p. 13):

> With Critical Theory overlaid on the Person-Centred Approach, I believe we have a better system to address diversity and multi-cultural issues. It also provides us with a coherent basis for social activism and advocacy.

In 1986, Rogers (see Kirschenbaum and Henderson 1990a: 138) made what may be seen as a sweeping claim for the person-centred approach. He wrote:

> The person-centered approach, then, is primarily a way of being that finds its expression in attitudes and behaviors that create a growth-promoting climate. It is a basic philosophy rather than simply a technique or a method. When this philosophy is lived, it helps the person

expand the development of his or her own capacities. When it is lived, it also stimulates constructive change in others. It empowers the individual, and when this personal power is sensed, experience shows that it tends to be used for personal and social transformation.

Certainly 'social change' became a focus for Rogers himself – he formulated views related to conflict resolution and the resolution of inter-cultural tensions and, in the last years of his life, was most interested in peace processes (see Barrett-Lennard 1998: 218–27). Sanford (1999: 13–28) gives an overview of groups she conducted with Rogers and others in areas of political tension including Dublin, Tbilisi, Witwatersrand and Moscow. But how does this claim that the person-centred approach is facilitative of social (and political) change measure up? Sanford (p. 26) believes that, while there has been some success, the full impact of the person-centred approach upon the world of politics is yet to come. An alternative but compatible view is that person-centred practitioners have lost contact with the political edge to the approach and the potential it has for social transformation. This is the position of Kearney (1997: 11). She believes that while (for example) gender issues and race issues have gradually come to be seen as relevant to therapy, class issues are ignored. She states (p. 12):

> I believe that most current person-centred counsellor training courses are highly selective in terms of which aspects of, for example Rogers' work, they choose to emphasise. Rogers himself saw person-centred counselling as having the potential to challenge and change the political structures as well as the internal structures which inhibit self-awareness and development. He considered that facilitating the client's opposition to those structures was and is a legitimate part of the therapeutic work of counsellors. I would go further and suggest that it is a responsibility of counsellors to be active in opposing those structures.

Cameron (1997: 16) too sees the political radicalism of Rogers as overlooked or even denied – 'Not only does Rogers seem to be largely unrecognised as politically radical, but is often critiqued, increasingly from within the person-centred world, as politically reactionary.' She challenges this view, especially as it is represented by claims that the actualising tendency is a 'modernist', ethnocentric and male-centred concept and that the person-centred approach is (from cross-cultural and feminist perspectives) charged with 'liberal individualism' and 'blaming the victim'. For both Kearney and Cameron, the shortfall is not in the person-centred approach but in its interpretation and application. I share their view that the political dimension of the approach is largely ignored or even deliberately avoided. There is a challenge here which person-centred practitioners as a whole have yet to meet.

Besides those person-centred writers on gender issues referred to above and Kearney and Cameron, there are, however, already those who frame their work in a political context. Keys (1999: 41–3), for example, discusses how the 'key concepts' of the Universal Declaration of Human Rights underpin her counselling practice and how these are consistent with person-centred theory. She considers that she is 'daily at the forefront of tackling human rights abuses and upholding the spirit of the Declaration through my work as a person-centred counsellor' (p. 47). Keys clearly sees a political dimension to her work.

3

The Underlying Epistemology: Outmoded Mid-Twentieth-Century Modernism?

The Philosophical/Psychological Basis for Person-Centred Counselling

The philosophical base of person-centred therapy and its relevance to a multi-cultural, twenty-first-century society has in itself been questioned and, surely, if the roots of the approach are not sound, then all its theory and practices are at least dubious? A defence against such accusations seems of primary importance.

There is an argument that, as a product of the American midwest writing in the mid-twentieth century, Rogers was in some way limited to a particular set of values and that, therefore, person-centred therapy preserves those limitations. Basically, the assumption is that the values of person-centred therapy are those of a postulated white, 'educated' middle class drawing on a Judaeo-Christian tradition, and that it places undue emphasis on 'American' concepts such as the importance of the individual over society in general, emphasising personal growth and personal indulgence over collective responsibility. So, far from being egalitarian and addressing people on their own terms as it claims, person-centred therapy privileges a particular world view, ignores 'cultural' differences, assumes the 'reality' of intangibles and seeks to impose its theoretical constructs on the experiences of people to whom they may be irrelevant or even alien. In this respect, person-centred therapy becomes the agent of a kind of cultural imperialism – in the eyes of its practitioners its values (explicit and implicit) are the norm to which all right-thinking people aspire and the therapist works (however unknowingly) towards the client's adoption of these values. In a way, this is a criticism of *any* approach to counselling or psychotherapy – see Masson (1992: 294–5) who refers to this tendency of clients to accept the values of the therapist – and I think there is a tendency on the part of therapists to see clients as 'cured' when they think like the therapist! Although person-centred theory requires practitioners of the approach to work with clients in a way which confirms their ways of being in the world, it may be that we need to be as much on our guard in this respect as any other therapist.

Leaving aside the fact that even if the first assertion that Rogers is 'culture-bound' is true (and, of course, we are all products of our experiences), it does not follow that the second is also true. Indeed, because, that person-centred therapy is similarly culture-bound, the subjective experience of the individual is central to person-centred therapy, it has the flexibility to adapt to the person and (perhaps less importantly) to the Zeitgeist. There are many currents other than those stemming from Rogers which have contributed to the tide which is the person-centred approach. Individuals from many 'cultures' (including those rooted in ethnicity, sexual orientation or religion) have thought about, applied, re-examined, re-interpreted or re-confirmed its basic principles, showing its relevance to them and the people with whom they work, so an explanation of the underlying epistemology of person-centred counselling and an exploration of its contemporary relevance seems worthwhile.

The person-centred approach has been described both as 'humanistic' and 'phenomenological', indeed Spinelli (1989: 159) sees person-centred theory and practices as drawing on both traditions. Briefly (drawing on Spinelli, 1994: 256–60) that it is 'humanistic' implies that person-centred therapy has the following foci:

- the client's current experience rather than past causes which may 'explain' that experience
- the totality of the client rather than a particular 'problem'
- the client's personal understanding and interpretation of their experience rather than the therapist's
- the client's freedom and ability to choose how to 'be'
- an egalitarian relationship between the client and the therapist
- the therapeutic relationship as intrinsically healing and/or growth-inspiring
- integration of self-concept and the 'self' *per se*
- the client's inherent actualising tendency and innately positive nature
- the client's core, unitary self as a source for individual development.

Spinelli (1989: 159) expresses the view that 'much of humanistic psychology appears to be largely culture-bound to the North American experience'. By implication, in at least as much as it is rooted in humanistic psychology, person-centred therapy and those who practise it, must be seen as similarly limited.

However, in a paper addressing the origins of client-centred therapy, Merry (1998: 96–103) argues that the principles of client-centred therapy were established *before* humanistic psychology emerged as a significant trend. It may be, then, that client-centred therapy helped shape humanistic psychology rather than the other way round. Also, along with other person-centred practitioners, I am doubtful that the principal characteristic of person-centred therapy is its 'humanistic' nature. I prefer to think of person-centred therapy as phenomenological and its key characteristic as the eschewing of power and expertise. This echoes Mearns and Thorne (2000: 27) who state:

> person-centred therapy ... does not in fact have much in common with the other established humanistic therapies. The governing feature of person-centred therapy (PCT) is not its 'humanistic' orientation but its forsaking of mystique and other 'powerful' behaviours of therapists. In this regard many humanistic therapies are as different from PCT as psychoanalysis.

Nevertheless, some of the arguments about humanistic approaches are seen by most people as relevant to a discussion of person-centred therapy.

Person-Centred Therapy and Postmodernism

Humanistic psychology is seen to have its roots in a twentieth-century, American view of human nature, and phenomenology draws principally on the work of Husserl and Heidegger who were products of nineteenth-century Europe. As indicated above, for some this leads to the assumption that the person-centred approach is somehow 'frozen', a product of a time long gone and an outdated philosophy. Leaving aside the absurdity of the underlying assumption that belief has a 'use-by' date (where would that leave the bulk of philosophical and metaphysical thought?), it is nevertheless worth considering person-centred theory in the light of the major epistemological trends of the later twentieth/early twenty-first centuries, and specifically postmodernism.

Postmodernism throws into question any universal claim including the concept of the self and, because the concept of a 'real', unitary self is, as shown above, at the heart of humanistic psychology, a postmodernist critique can be seen as striking at the core of person-centred therapy (see Jones 1996). Jones (pp. 19–20) places Rogers firmly in the modernist school in that 'person-centred theory asserts that it has discovered generalizable truths about our psychological make-up'. O'Hara (1995: 47) on the other hand refers to Rogers as 'the unwitting postmodernist pioneer', claiming that as early as the 1950s he was grappling 'with some of the most puzzling philosophical questions of this century'. These she characterises thus:

- Is knowledge of the human world equivalent to knowledge of the natural world?
- In these post-Heisenberg times, is the idea of value-free objectivity realistic in even the physical sciences, let alone human sciences?
- What is the relationship of the knower to the known?
- What is the relationship between an insider's knowledge and an outsider's?
- What is the purpose of human inquiry – understanding or prediction and control?
- Do the established scientific ways of asking questions determine the kind of answers that may be generated?
- How can we do holistic contextual research and still make sense of our data?

It may be that, as in so many other areas, it is not possible to squeeze Rogers and person-centred theory into a particular camp. On the one hand, Rogers was trained in the scientific method and was pioneering (even revolutionary) in applying that to understanding the psychotherapeutic process; on the other, he apparently became dissatisfied with positivism as a way of achieving a comprehension of the human condition. As O'Hara indicates, this is clearly so in the 1950s when Rogers (1959: 251) wrote:

There is a widespread feeling in our group that the logical positivism in which we were professionally reared is not necessarily the final philosophical word in an area in which the phenomenon of subjectivity plays such a vital and central part ... Is there some view, possibly developing out of an existentialist orientation, which might ... find more room for the existing subjective person ...?

In 1968 (in Kirschenbaum and Henderson 1990a: 265), Rogers wrote 'I like to create hypotheses and I like to test them against hard reality' – surely the statement of a positivist and far from the postmodern position O'Hara attributes to him. But in the same paper (p. 268) he writes:

If it seems hard or difficult to give up the certainty of knowing which has customarily been related to science, perhaps we should recognise that the statements I am making put a firm emphasis upon science as a *process* [original emphasis], rather than upon science as a result.

This gives credence to O'Hara's view as does Rogers' chapter 'Do we need 'a' reality?' (1980: 96–108). By 1985 (see Kirschenbaum and Henderson, 1990a: 281) Rogers is arguing 'the need for a new science'. He (pp. 281–5) writes of his 'pleasant surprise' at reading of 'new models of science that are more appropriate to a human science', mentioning the work of Reason and Rowan (1981), Douglass and Moustakas (1985) and Mearns and McLeod (1984) among others. The latter paper he regarded as important because of its emphasis on the collaborative nature of research. In his (pp. 284–5) analysis of the common elements of these new approaches, he includes an understanding that Newtonian science is simply one form of science – others are equally valid; that we can never gain *certain* knowledge, that is, truth is subjective; and, most importantly:

A further point of agreement is that there is no one method that is best. The methodology chosen must be appropriate to the question being asked. That is very important, because, if taken seriously, it will prevent new rigidities from developing.

Implicit in this statement is that 'knowledge' depends on the approach and nature of the knower – that is, that there is not some objective truth out there waiting to be discovered, but that meaning is constructed (or perhaps more importantly, co-constructed). This seems not too far from a postmodern position. I think this supports my belief that it is a mistake to attempt to pigeon-hole Rogers or the person-centred approach. The latter is by its very nature responsive and adaptive rather than dogmatic, and although my assertion that 'dogma is the enemy of the person-centred approach' (Wilkins 2000a: 35) has been criticised (by an anonymous referee) as in itself dogmatic (and I accept the criticism but can see no way round the apparent paradox), there is some essential quality underlying the person-centred approach which means it is somehow 'open'. Open to new ideas, open to 'horses for courses', open to the multiplicity of truths. But does this mean it is essentially postmodern? Ellingham (1999: 62–78) offers a critique of the 'postmodernist porridge' and advances a scholarly argument which demonstrates why it is in error to view the person-centred approach in these terms. I take the view that it is probably mistaken to attempt to 'fix' the person-centred approach and it is certainly mistaken to believe that Rogers is its only theorist and that his word is in some sense 'sacred'. And yet this is done so often. Outsiders take some notion of what was said (probably in the 1940s or 1950s), remove it from its contemporary context and isolate it from the following 40-plus years of development and reconsideration and offer a criticism which is therefore limited.

Insiders tend to base arguments for their personal beliefs and practices on the precedent of Rogers. Now, Rogers said so much in so many ways over such a long time, it is nearly always possible to find *something* which can be construed as supporting one argument and refuting another – it is a bit like interpreting a religious text (and I am aware of the implications of this statement – in a way I am pointing out the dangers of attributing authority and perhaps even infallibility to Rogers). Although something of the essence of his belief remained unchanged, it is mistaken, even insulting, to assume that a revolutionary thinker such as Rogers did not change, develop and grow in over 60 years of professional life although I accept Bozarth's (1998: 10–11) contention that the *fundamentals* were constant. It is equally mistaken to take Rogers as the *only* person-centred theorist of note. The development of person-centred theory did not stop with the death of Rogers in 1987 and even before that time many other people had made significant contributions to it. Areas in which these advances have been made include:

- The 'classic client-centred' approach which has been illuminated, refined, interpreted or expanded upon by (for example) Shlien (1984), Bozarth (1990), Brodley (1990) and Mearns (1996).
- Additions to the person-centred 'family' of therapies (perhaps most importantly 'experiential therapy' growing from the work of Gendlin 1978).
- Spiritual aspects and implications of person-centred counselling have been explored (see, for example, Grant 1995; Thorne 1996; and Purton, 1998).
- Cross-cultural relevance has been queried (by, for example, Holdstock 1990, 1993) and demonstrated (see, for example, Morotomi 1998).
- Application to the arena of creative therapies has been explored and explained (see N. Rogers 1985; Silverstone 1994; Wilkins 1994a).
- Relevance in the broad area of gender and sexuality has been examined (see Natiello 1980/1999; Galgut 1999; and Warner 1999).
- Theoretical concepts have been re-argued and re-evaluated by practitioners belonging to a variety of what Warner (1998/1999) sees as the tribes which constitute the person-centred nation.

These views (and many more) are explored in subsequent chapters.

There are other discourses which question, throw light on or cast doubt on some of the concepts which are apparently inherent to person-centred therapy. For example, the self, awareness, consciousness are all terms commonly used in the language of psychotherapy and many of the processes described in that discourse depend upon an acceptance of their 'reality' – but these very notions are questionable. Sampson (1989: 13–15) 'deconstructs' these ideas and shows how Derrida questions psychological understandings of 'personhood' and 'consciousness'. Sampson offers a critique of the Western concept of 'persons as more or less integrated universes and distinctive wholes' (p. 14). Parker (1989: 65) describes the 'old paradigm' of experimental social psychology as an attempt to 'break the mental processes of individuals into measurable and manipulable components' and sees this as 'part of the power pattern of contemporary society'. Basing his reasoning on the work of Foucault, he concludes (p. 68) that:

> If we really want to break out of the cultural assumptions that under-pinned the 'old paradigm', we need to be even more uncertain about agency and the self. We need, in fact, to ask how the self is implicated moment by moment, through the medium of discourse, in power.

Parker's argument is as applicable to psychotherapy (and therefore person-centred therapy) as it is to social psychology.

A colleague who bases his ideas in postmodernism and discourse analysis, said to me in the course of this writing (and I heard this almost as if it were an accusation), 'you think emotions have an ontological reality'. This I take as a criticism of my adherence to the person-centred approach rather than as a personal attack. Do I think that emotions are real? Is this implicit in the person-centred approach? In response to the criticism I thought about this. Yes, in a sense I do think emotions are 'real'. This is because I value the subjective experience of persons as to what is 'true'. If someone attributes to themselves an emotion or accepts the attribution of another then that emotion for that person, in that time and place, is real. This does rise directly out of person-centred theory (although I suspect that for me the realisation was the other way round). Clearly, there are other views.

Person-Centred Therapy, the Self, Chaos Theory and the New Physics

From the perspective of an entirely different discourse, that of the 'new physics', Zohar (1990) proposes a model of the self which is different from that normally believed to underlie approaches to psychotherapy. She demonstrates that quantum mechanics casts doubt on the feasibility of Cartesian dualism, but she does validate the concept of 'I' and the reality of relationships. She writes (p. 108):

Understood quantum mechanically we see the self as a fluctuating and fuzzy thing whose boundaries, both internal and external, are always shifting and changing. It is none the less a real thing, a substantial thing. The self is not an illusion.

This resonates with the person-centred notion of the 'self' as a process rather than a fixed entity (see, for example, Rogers 1967: 27; Ellingham 1997: 53; van Kalmthout 1998: 99). This notion also underpins my thinking in (for example) Wilkins (1997c: 19) where I argue that 'the "self" must arise from a process and not merely within an individual but from interpersonal and transpersonal processes too'. Interestingly, Bozarth (1985: 179–82) offers an understanding of the person-centred approach in terms of quantum theory and points out that the person-centred paradigm is not only consistent with 'modern physics' but also with mystical thought. For Sanford (1993: 253–73) the comparison is with 'the theory of chaos'. For example, in the work of Prigogine, the Nobel chemistry laureate, on 'open systems', Sanford (pp. 257–9) finds parallels with Rogers' ideas about the actualising tendency and draws extensively on Gleick's 1987 work *Chaos: Making of a New Science* to establish similarities between person-centred theory and modern physics.

Zohar also writes about 'sub-selves' (1990: 114–15):

Like elementary particle systems, we too – our personalities, our selves – are quantum systems. Within any one individual, the physics of over-lapping sub-selves can easily be seen as the overlapping wave patterns within the Bose-Einstein condensate of consciousness. Each of us as a person is a composite of quantum sub-selves which are also one self (one highest unity).

Although Zohar's preferred comparison seems to be with Kleinian and object relations ideas, there is a resonance here with the sub-personalities to which I refer in Wilkins (1993) and Mearns (1999: 125–30) concept of 'configurations of self'.

The Problem of the 'Self'

Although the 'organism' is in many ways more important in person-centred theory (see Rogers 1951: 484–8; Rogers 1959: 221; Barrett-Lennard 1998: 74–6; Tudor and Merry 2002: 91–3), and Tudor and Merry state that person-centred theory may justifiably be considered as an *organismic* (as distinct from a self-) psychology (2002: 92), it is the notion of the self which has attracted more attention. There are critiques as to the nature of self within the person-centred tradition. For example, Holdstock (1993: 229–52) reconsiders what he sees as the centrality of the self and autonomy of the individual which is embedded in person-centred theory and (p. 230) offers an alternative which

hints at the possibility of a concept of the person which challenges the monocultural notion of the self as a demarcated entity, set off against the world. In this newer view, the self is considered to be inextricably intertwined with other people. The extended concept of the self may even include the deceased as well as the larger universe of animals, plants and inanimate objects. Power and control are not considered to rest predominantly with the individual but within the field of forces within which the individual exists.

Holdstock's ideas are interesting and what he writes about (feminist notions of the self and the self from a transcultural perspective) has contributed to person-centred theory, but I wonder if he is returning to an earlier person-centred position rather than setting forth a new one? Rogers explains that he originally believed that the self 'was a vague, ambiguous, scientifically meaningless term' but that his clinical experience showed him that people spoke of their 'self' as if it was an entity – 'it seemed clear ... that the self was an important element in the experience of the client' (1959: 200–1). To me, it seems that Zohar echoes this view. Rogers (pp. 202–3) shows how an operational definition of 'self' was reached via a cyclical process of clinical observation, conceptualisation and research. It would be a mistake to think that as a result of this observation, thought and research Rogers arrived at a conclusion that there was an objective, 'thing-like', fixed entity to which the label 'self' could be attached. Van Kalmthout (1998: 59) shows that Rogers accentuated the fluidity and flexibility of the self and Rogers (1967: 27) himself writes, 'life, at its best, is a flowing, changing process in which nothing is fixed'. For me, what all this means is that the self is central to person-centred theory *because* people describe themselves as having a self – there is an inevitable circularity here! Moreover, the nature of the self people describe changes from moment to moment and certainly from year to year. If I am right and the person-centred theoretical concept of the self is drawn from descriptions of subjective experience, then there is nothing to stop it including the concepts of other cultures and discourses. Thus, in terms of person-centred theory, 'self' can embrace the 'fluidity of the self–other boundary' referred to by Holdstock (1993: 243). A person's self is whatever he or she believes it to be. It can be internal and detached, a 'thing' riding round in a body, it can include ancestors – even the physical boundaries of a community – for example, the rocks at a village entrance – embrace transpersonal or spiritual connections or something else entirely. Whatever their personal beliefs, person-centred practitioners are charged with responding to other persons as they perceive themselves to be. The mistake would be to act on the assumption that the client conceptualises 'self' in the same way as the therapist. In my view, in terms of classic person-centred theory, whatever the self is, it is still subject to the actualising tendency (because it is a universal force acting on all living things); or, if 'self' extends to the physical and metaphysical, then the formative tendency is the operating force. Mearns and Thorne (2000: 187–9) question the universality of the actualising tendency asking if it is 'culturally bounded' (p. 187). They take they view that it is difficult to come to a conclusion about this either way because 'there can be no fixed cultural perspective from which to define reality' (p. 188). In a way, this is an incontestable statement but what if, just as 'self' means different things in different cultural contexts, each culture defines the actualising and formative tendencies in their own terms? A simple definition of the actualising tendency would be *the tendency of life forms to develop more complex organisation and to fulfil their potential.* Mearns and Thorne (2000: 181), appreciating the 'simple elegance' of the actualising tendency as the single motivating force, state 'there is logic in the notion that there should be a fundamental drive in life to maintain, develop and enhance the functioning of the organism and that this tendency can manifest itself in many different guises'. Could it be that the universal applicability of the actualising tendency is at this 'biological' level, and that it is value-free at least in the sense that it is neither 'good' nor 'bad'? If so, cultural differences come into the interpretation – for example what is 'constructive' in human nature may very well be contentious. Maybe this thinking is too loose and results in relatively meaningless concepts. Mearns and Thorne (2000: 177–86), however, offer a solution to the cultural applicability of self-theory in their dialogical framework for a person-centred theory of the self. They discuss 'the whole *actualising process* which contains not only the actualising tendency but the dialogue between it and the restraints of social mediation' (p. 181). This leads them to four propositions which, in terms of person-centred theory, describe a dialogical conception of the self. These propositions (after Mearns and Thorne 2000: 181–4) are:

- The actualising tendency is the sole motivational force.
- The promptings of the actualising tendency inspire their own resistance within the social life space of the person. An interim term for this resistance is the force of 'social mediation'.

- A psychological 'homeostasis' develops where the balance is under 'dual control', with the drive of the actualising tendency and the restraint of the social imperative both able to exercise power.

- Disorder' is caused when the person becomes chronically stuck within his own process so that the homeostatic balance cannot reconfigure to respond to changing circumstances.

There is a necessary and productive tension between the actualising tendency and the force of social mediation, and

[t]here will be times when the pressure of the actualising tendency will inspire resistance. Such resistance is intimately related both to the actualising tendency and to the person's current existence as a social being. The effect of the resistance serves to maintain a balance which allows for a degree of expression for the actualising tendency while taking care to preserve the viability of the social context within the person's 'life space'....
The forces of social mediation form a coherent and functional part of our existence as social beings, allowing us expression of the actualising tendency but exerting an imperative which cautions against endangering of the social life space. (Mearns and Thorne 2000: 182–3)

Because of this, it is incumbent upon person-centred therapists to be equally attentive to both parts of the dynamic or, in the words of Mearns and Thorne (2000: 114), to both 'growthful' and 'not-for-growth' configurations of the self.

If person-centred theory can not be easily 'pigeon-holed' and if it has greater flexibility than some of its critics allow, then the relevance of person-centred therapy to clients from a range of cultural backgrounds is hard to dismiss on theoretical grounds alone, as is its contemporary aptness. Because at its heart is the imperative to respond to the client's subjective experience rather than to impose the theoretical constructs of the therapist, the accusation that person-centred therapy is 'culture bound' falls away. This does not mean that person-centred practitioners can rest on their laurels, content in the knowledge that, fundamentally, their theory is adaptable to many people, many situations. Rather we are called upon to address constantly our own ways of conceptualising the world, taking note of the ideas of others. Perhaps the greatest value of the work of (for example) Holdstock (1993) and Zohar (1990) is to draw attention to these different ways of experiencing the world and different explanations for phenomena such as the 'self'.

4
The Model of the Person:
An Insufficient Base?

The person-centred approach has been criticised as lacking a theory of personality and, in particular, of child development and thus as having an inadequate view of how (for example) neuroses and psychoses may arise. This charge immediately raises two questions: first, is it true? Second, does it matter one way or the other? Perhaps this criticism is made most strongly by therapists of a psychodynamic orientation. For example, Wheeler (in Wheeler and McLeod 1995: 286) airs two 'serious reservations' about person-centred therapy. The first concerns the assumption of inherent human goodness (a view addressed in the following chapter) and the other is that there 'is the lack of theory of human growth and development to underpin the practice, and [a] subsequent disregard for assessment'. This 'lack' is also apparent to at least some people within the person-centred tradition. Cain (1993: 135–6) asserts that:

> Rogers' (1959) theory of personality and psychotherapy is an elegant but rudimentary theory that barely addresses the issue of how personality develops. It provides very little help in understanding the wide varieties of disturbing and pathological experiences and behaviors (e.g., depression, obsessive-compulsive behavior, disturbed body image) that render people dysfunctional to varying degrees. Neither does it offer much help for the counsellor in providing even tentative guidelines regarding how therapists might respond differentially to various forms of psychopathology.

This 'rudimentary theory' and what may seem an obsessive resistance to 'labelling' is in turn seen as leading to a disregard for assessment which may result in inappropriate therapy contracts and thus waste the client's time and money – or (in extreme cases?) actually damage the client. Those who take this view are therefore likely to be critical of the lack of 'professionalism' of person-centred practitioners because they are seen as shirking this responsibility towards their clients.

Is There a Practical 'Need' for a Theory of the Origins of 'Incongruence'?

The second of Rogers' (1957) 'necessary and sufficient' conditions is that the person in the client role is 'in a state of incongruence, being vulnerable or anxious'. That is, incongruence, the misalignment of inner and outer ways of being (that is the organism and the self-concept) or the disharmony between them is at the root of any 'dysfunction' (although this dysfunction always has a 'usefulness' to the individual perhaps in a way similar to Freudian defence mechanisms). Barrett-Lennard (1998: 77) puts it thus:

> Denial to awareness implies that certain behaviours and/or inner states of the person are not recognised as *self*-experiences, and in this sense not owned by the individual and not organized into his or her self-picture. The resulting *incongruence* between self and experience, involves a state of 'vulnerability' and a degree of dysfunction. However, its effect is also to minimize conscious inner conflict and anxiety.

Tengland (2001: 159–73) explores the links between incongruence and mental health and (p. 169) defines incongruence as contributing to 'ill health' 'since it often reduces the person's ability to reach vital goals'. Although incongruence may contribute to ill health, it is worth remembering that the second of Rogers' conditions for constructive personality change requires that client incongruence manifests as vulnerability or anxiety. Wilkins and Bozarth (2001: ix–x) point out that vulnerability and anxiety are products of incongruence and not its causes. We questioned whether it is possible to be incongruent without being vulnerable and anxious and, if so, did this mean that sometimes therapy is contra-indicated even for an incongruent client? Rogers (1959: 215) reports a study of Gallagher as indicating 'that less anxious clients tend never to become involved in therapy, but drop out'. Considering this, Wilkins and Bozarth (2001: x) state:

> Whether these less anxious clients are actually more congruent and therefore less in need of unconditional positive regard from another, or unaware of their incongruence is hard to know. But perhaps it is irrelevant. Does condition two imply that therapy will only be successful if, in some way and on some level, the person in the client role is sufficiently aware of and troubled by incongruence to persist in the endeavour? Almost certainly.

In person-centred theory, there *are* explanations for how incongruence may arise and why it is undesirable. Wilkins and Bozarth (2001: ix) consider incongruence as the product of 'conditions of worth' and state that incongruence is undesirable, for example, because it is incompatible with the state of being 'fully functioning'. We state that 'incongruence can be viewed as arising from a lack of (or insufficient) unconditional positive regard'. Incongruence may operate through the defence mechanisms of distortion and denial but how, if at all, does this impinge on practice?

For 'constructive personality change to occur' (Rogers 1957: 96), the practice of person-centred therapy (actually, any psychotherapy, for Rogers, was making an integrative statement, not defining person-centred therapy) requires that the six conditions exist and continue over a period of time. There is no need for anything else. While (for example) empathy may require the counsellor to have and communicate an understanding of the client's internal frame of reference, an appreciation of the origins of the client's way of being is not required. At least in terms of classical client-centred therapy, how the therapist behaves towards the client is the same whatever the cause of their incongruence. Also, by definition, person-centred therapy is concerned with the current subjective experience of clients, not with their history (because only the present is accessible). Of course, one of the things available in the present is the remembrance or *perception* of the past. These are part of the client's current subjective experience and so are the stuff of person-centred therapy. If it is how clients perceive themselves *now* that matters (for they are the experts), then of what use is the counsellor's 'knowledge' of the roots of their incongruence? Indeed, could an hypothesis as to the reasons why a client feels and acts as they do be counter-therapeutic? Certainly, for therapists to form views based upon theory, past experience or whatever else other than what the client tells them is potentially misleading, even dangerous. This is because it may lead therapists to impose their own frames of reference on the interaction and, convinced of their 'knowledge', cease to pay attention to the client's understanding. In a way, from a person-centred position, it does not even matter that the therapist is 'right' about causal factors if the client takes a different view – it is what the client believes, considers to be relevant or 'knows' that is important and only that. So, in terms of person-centred theory (at least from a classical perspective), the cause of incongruence is largely irrelevant to practice and perhaps this is especially true with respect to 'assessment'.

Person-centred therapists tend to react badly to the notion of assessment, perhaps because it is heard as a synonym for 'diagnosis' and there is presumed to be an implication that it results in a treatment plan of some kind. Feltham (2000: 412) encapsulates this attitude, writing:

Broadly speaking, most practitioners of humanistic and existential therapies are opposed to psychodiagnostic concepts and procedures on the grounds of *inaccuracy, gratuitousness, stigmatization, disempowerment, abuse* and *'shrinkage'* (this last colloquialism referring to the tendency of psychiatric labels to shrink or reduce the totality of the human being to a spuriously named *part* of themselves, to dissect them psychologically and treat them accordingly).

Diagnosis and treatment plans are antipathetic to person-centred therapy *because* it is assumed they arise from the frame of reference and 'expertise' of the therapist and do not necessarily reflect the experience and needs of the client (but see below for an alternative understanding of assessment as a mutual process). For the therapist to proceed on the basis of an assessment of this kind may, therefore, be a mistake – indeed it is likely to be. Perhaps an illustration from my own practice will illuminate this (here, as elsewhere, when I refer to case material, confidentiality is preserved by making a 'composite' – biographical details are disguised and I may draw on two or more encounters but the *process* is as given).

I was young and innocent in the ways of counselling when Margaret came to see me and my head was full of theories and ideas about the nature of human beings and how their various miseries might arise. Margaret was from Africa and the tale she told me was of multiple loss – the loss of a child, the death of a much-loved uncle, the breakdown of a loving relationship and of being far from her supportive village community, lost and alone in a foreign land. Margaret was obviously grieving. I knew about grief. All I had to do was to get her to talk to me about the people and places she had lost, see her safely through the stages of grieving and she would be fine – still sad of course but better able to function and to get on with her life.

Unfortunately, Margaret had not read the same books as me. We sat week after week and she would not talk to me about her baby, her uncle, her partner or her friends and relations. I knew she 'ought' to but at least (in terms of the approach to which I was developing an affinity), I knew enough not to cajole her. Our sessions were for the most part silent. We would exchange a few words at the beginning, I would remind her of the time about half way through and towards the end. The most Margaret would do was to look up and smile sadly. On the one hand, I was saying to myself, 'I know about silence, silence is OK, I can cope with silence – all I have to do is be here'; on the other, my self-dialogue was, 'She still hasn't got to grips with her grief, I must be doing something wrong, I'm a useless counsellor. There must be something I should be doing.'

> *Eventually, at the end of a session Margaret told me that she would not be coming any more – she was now too busy. This convinced me that she had got nothing from our relationship and that I had failed her. I did not feel at all good about that. Some weeks later, Margaret sought me out, bringing me a gift. She told me that I had been wonderful, without me she would not have survived in England, would not have advanced in her profession. I was apparently the best thing since sliced bread. I was glad to hear this but really quite mystified!*

Over the years, I have given a great deal of thought to my relationship with Margaret. I learnt a lot from it. My attempt to impose my understanding of her needs on Margaret could have been disastrous. That I was 'person-centred enough' to stay with her experience (at least to a sufficient extent) comforts me. But I still do not understand exactly what that experience was. I *think* that in those long silences she was journeying back to Africa and that somehow I was her companion and that this was important. But I do not know that this is true and I shall almost certainly never know. Although, at the time, I had not a clue what was happening for Margaret, she seems to have found some usefulness in our relationship – this was apparently quite independent of a need for my understanding of the root causes of her difficulties. It seems that she required no particular strategies on my part, merely that I was attentive to her in her process – that is, that I communicated the 'therapist conditions' (those of Rogers' 'necessary and sufficient conditions' which describe the therapist's attributes). In this, I was at least moderately successful. She did whatever else was needed.

What is important in terms of person-centred theory and practice about this story is that my 'assessment' of Margaret, although possibly accurate in one sense, was totally immaterial in another and that I have found an explanation for her behaviour and appreciation, the function of which seems to be to make me feel better. From my reflections on this experience, I suggest that, in a way, the therapist's theoretical understanding of the client's incongruence may be irrelevant to the client's experience in the therapeutic relationship (and may even be counter-therapeutic unless deliberate attempts are made to set it on one side). This is consistent with person-centred theory.

However, an understanding of the roots of disturbance and human development in general (and perhaps speculation about individual clients) can be helpful because it is in some way enabling of the therapist (perhaps as a means of dealing with doubts and fears or even just 'scratching the itch of curiosity'), but the place for such theorising is in private reflection and/or supervision – theorising may inform practice but it should not dictate it. For example, when I speculate about the reasons why clients are as they are, I think it may sometimes help me towards extending unconditional positive regard to them (see Wilkins 2000a: 27–8 for a 'case-work' illustration of how this might come about). It also alerts me to the possibility that they may subtly tell me of some experience difficult to relate (such as abuse or a 'shameful' act) and so I am more likely to pick up signals and respond to hints. Lastly, such speculation allows me to deal with my need to solve problems, to 'know'. I like doing crosswords and playing bridge and there is something about reaching a conclusion about the causes of a client's behaviour which is similarly satisfying. Because this is my need and because I know that I can be wrong, it is important that I do this in my own time and that I do not act as if my conclusions are accurate. The danger against which I have constantly to guard is that I assume the correctness and appropriateness of my conclusions, at least to the extent that I cease to hear the client's alternative 'explanations' – that is, I somehow dismiss anything the client says which does not fit my pre-formulated view. When I put all this together it seems that not only is there no practical need for person-centred therapists to form a view as to the root causes of the incongruence of their clients, but to do so may be unwise. All that said, person-centred theory *does* centre around a model of the person which includes a theory of human development and how emotional disturbance may arise. And, given the reservations I express above, an understanding of this is helpful to practice.

The Person-Centred Model of the Person

Cain's opinion that Rogers' (1959: 221–3) theory of personality is rudimentary is by no means universally held. Barrett-Lennard (1998: 77) refers to that paper as 'Rogers' major formulation of theory', and Raskin (1996: 14) calls it 'the most rigorous exposition of Rogers' theories'. Rogers (1959: 221–3) considers the following aspects of personality:

- postulated characteristics of the human infant
- the development of the self
- the need for positive regard
- the development of the need for self-regard
- the development of conditions of worth

- the development of incongruence between self and experience
- the development of discrepancies in behaviour
- the experience of threat and the process of defence
- the process of breakdown and disorganisation
- the process of reintegration
- specification of functional relationships in the theory of personality.

Rogers (pp. 232–3) goes on to consider the evidence from research for his theory of personality. On the face of it, there is little about the human organism that this theory does not explain. It traces both 'healthy' development and 'dysfunctional' development and shows how there may be a progression from the latter back to the former. Whether the person-centred explanation of the human condition is accepted or not may be more a question of 'faith' and personal preference of the therapist than its susceptibility to 'proof'. Even with its early emphasis on research and the derivation of theory from practice, many people would see a belief in the principles of client-centred therapy as just that – a belief, a faith. Rogers' theory is derived from psychotherapeutic practice and it is succinctly stated but, as I have written elsewhere (Wilkins 1997a: 41), 'a theory that is simply stated is not necessarily an inconsequential theory'.

To return to Wheeler's concern about an absence of a theory of child development, some person-centred practitioners have been aware of this apparent lack and have sought to address it. Drawing on Rogers' six necessary and sufficient conditions, Biermann-Ratjen (1996: 13) offers the necessary conditions for self-development in early childhood. These are:

1. That the baby is in *contact* with a significant other.
2. That the baby is preoccupied with *evaluating experience* which might possibly arouse *anxiety*.
3. That the *significant other person* is *congruent in the relationship* to the baby, does not experience anything inconsistent with her self-concept while in contact with the baby when it is preoccupied with evaluating his experience.
4. That the significant other is *experiencing unconditional positive regard* toward the baby's processes of evaluating his experience.
5. That the significant other is *experiencing an empathic under-standing* of the baby's experiencing within his *internal frame of reference.*
6. That the baby gradually *perceives* both the unconditional positive regard of the significant other person for him and the empathic understanding so that in the baby's *awareness* there is gradually *a belief or prognosis* that the unconditionally positively regarding and empathically understanding object would when reacting to other experiences of the baby also exhibit positive regard and empathic understanding.

She then states (p. 14) 'positive regard is the precondition for self development'. Later in this paper, Biermann-Ratjen explains the implications of her model of child development for psychopathology (person-centred understandings of psychopathology are returned to below in Chapter 8). She also compares her conclusion from person-centred theory with those of therapists of other orientations (specifically Sullivan and the attachment theorists, including Bowlby) and reaches the conclusion that '[client-centred psychotherapists'] assumptions on how a self-concept comes about, with its intrinsic links to relating to others, are shared by researchers in other fields and have scientific backing' (Biermann-Ratjen 1998: 112–13). Clearly, it is possible to understand child development in terms of the person-centred model.

Person-Centred Therapy, 'Transference' and the Unconscious

Another area in which person-centred theory is seen by some to be lacking is with respect to the 'phenomenon' of transference. Tobin (1991: 18) in his comparison of psychoanalytic self psychology and person-centred therapy writes:

> Rogers believed, somewhat naively in my opinion, that he could avoid transference phenomena simply by being congruent and non-authoritarian with clients. For example, he endorses the idea that transference is caused by a therapist taking an evaluative stance with a client.

In this analysis, person-centred therapists are seen as encouraging, through their actions and approach, positive transference (being supportive and 'parental' in the best sense of the word) but denying the client the necessary expression of 'negative' transference feelings. This prevents real in-depth therapy. The 'discouragement of negative transference' argument seems to be rooted in the assumption that being person-centred somehow means being bland and 'nice', but, in context, confrontation and challenge may be part of the process of therapy. Person-centred therapy depends (among other things) on the expression of real feelings *in the moment* and this can very easily include anger at the therapist.

It is largely true that person-centred theorists tend to be dismissive of transference. For us, either transference may (sometimes) be part of an interaction but to 'work' with it would be counter-therapeutic, or it is an artefact of the psychoanalytic mind-set and has no reality.

Rogers (see Kirschenbaum and Henderson 1990a: 129–30) acknowledged the existence of 'emotions which have little or no relationship to the therapist's behaviour' but saw them as of little practical relevance. He wrote:

> In the therapeutic interaction, all of these attitudes – positive or negative, 'transference' feelings, or therapist-caused reactions – are best dealt with in the same way. If the therapist is sensitively understanding and genuinely acceptant and non-judgmental, therapy will move forward *through* these feelings. There is absolutely no need to make a special case of attitudes that are transferred to the therapist, and no need for the therapist to permit the dependence that is so often a part of other forms of therapy, particularly psychoanalysis. It is entirely possible to accept dependent feelings, without permitting the client to change the therapist's role.

Other person-centred theorists have offered alternative models for the process described as 'transference', perhaps most notable of these being Shlien's (1984: 153–81) 'countertheory of transference' which he intended to be instrumental in developing an alternative theory of the unconscious. In this paper, Shlien (p. 153) asserts 'transference is a fiction, invented and maintained by the therapist to protect himself from the consequences of his own behaviour'. Brodley (1997: 2) takes issue with what she sees as a tendency to take psychoanalytic concepts as if they were 'real' and the theory from which they are derived as having a particular validity. She writes: 'Neither is true. Psychoanalytic theory has not been proved. Nor has any other theory.' This strikes me as important. 'Transference' is a term used by some people to describe a process they observe and to which they attribute significance. It is a concept, not the process and, if this process occurs at all, there are alternative explanations for it. These include person-centred explanations. It is also possible that person-centred practitioners observe the same processes as therapists of other orientations but name and understand them differently. In Wilkins (1997b: 38), for example, I point out that some of the (many) processes described as 'countertransference' may, in terms of person-centred theory, be described as empathy. There is no reason to suppose that psychoanalytic theory has greater validity than person-centred theory. Indeed it is the person-centred case that, from the outset, person-centred theory has been tested through research and the close examination of actual therapy sessions in a way in which psychoanalytic theory has not. In his last theoretical paper, Rogers (1987: 182–8) challenged psychoanalysts to provide evidence that working with 'transference neurosis' is important to successful therapy. Clearly, he thought that this challenge was unlikely to be accepted. He wrote (pp. 187–8):

> Why the reluctance to make known what actually happens in the therapist's dealings with this core of the analytic process? ... The questions cannot be finally answered until psychoanalysts are willing to open their work to professional scrutiny.

Lietaer (1993: 35) represents another person-centred view when he responds to Shlien, writing:'Yes, John, there is a transference.' He goes on to state (p. 36):

> In client-centred therapy, too, the client repeats his past in his relationship with the therapist. But the way it is dealt with is partly different from the psychoanalytic orientation. Firstly, there is the belief that certain transference reactions – which can be viewed as security measures on the part of the client – will gradually melt away without explicit working through under the beneficial effect of a good working alliance. Secondly, client-centred therapy does not provide a *priority in principle* [original emphasis] to working with a problem in the here-and-now relationship with the therapist.

So, it is not that person-centred practitioners are ignorant of transference phenomena but that we have an alternative explanation for them and different ideas about the relevance of 'transference' attitudes to practice. Rogers did accept the notion of the unconscious (see, for example, Kirschenbaum and Henderson 1990a: 270) but it is true that he did not attach the same importance to it as do psychoanalytic theorists. In person-centred theory, there is no acceptance of the unconscious as a repository of repressed functions and primitive drives or desires. Thorne (1992a: 82) records that Rogers does not ignore the unconscious and did accept it as a reality. He writes:

> Rogers would assuredly claim that his respect for the unconscious compels him to refrain from adopting any map of this essentially unknowable terrain which might lead him to impose his view or interpretation on his client.

This applies not only to 'transference' but to all other 'unconscious' processes. Subsequent person-centred thinkers have re-addressed the unconscious (see, for example, Coulson 1995; Ellingham 1997; and Wilkins 1997d). These writers tend to take the view that there is a constant flow between the 'conscious' and the 'unconscious' and suggest a process model for the human mind as opposed to a model which proposes a particular structure. Whatever the nature of the unconscious, for the person-centred therapist what matters is that therapy does not stray into it but remains centred on the current awareness and experience of the client. Mearns and Thorne (2000: 175–6) offer an expansion of the self to include subceived or 'edge of awareness' material but are clear that this does not include the unconscious. They believe that to stay with the client's awareness and emerging awareness does not amount to a naive limitation (because of a presumed 'wealth of material to be uncovered within the unconscious') but that their belief (and, by implication, that of other person-centred practitioners) is actually well-considered and well-founded. They write (p. 176):

> Much is lost by disappearing into the unconscious. By definition we have entered areas which cannot yet be known by the client and where, also by definition, the client cannot be 'expert'. From the person-centred perspective, operating from a therapeutic frame where the client cannot be expert in relation to his existence brings enormous dangers of disempowerment, which at best may hugely lengthen the therapeutic process and at worst may further externalise the client's locus of evaluation. The unconscious world of the client as it is 'explored' in therapy is, in fact, a combination of the *therapist's* theoretical constructions and the *therapist's* imagination.

The Importance of Theory to Practice

But how important is a theory of personality to the *practice* of person-centred therapy? My first and instinctive answer is 'hardly at all' – although I immediately want to qualify that statement. One of the most important implications of all person-centred theory is that practice takes precedence over theory (another necessary paradox!). From the outset, theory was derived from practice, not the other way round. This remains true. In the therapeutic encounter it is the client's subjective understanding of themselves, the world, and the therapist which matters most, not the therapist's theoretical under-standing. It may be that the client's aggressive impulses can be understood in terms of conditions of worth but in the moment of relating this is unimportant. What the therapist must do is under-stand (empathise with) and accept (offer unconditional positive regard with respect to) the aggressive impulses and the feelings, thoughts and sensations which accompany them, while being true to him or herself (congruent). All other things are put from the thera-pist's mind – certainly to interpret the client's behaviour in terms of theory would detract from tracking the client's experience and there-fore be counter-therapeutic. However, I share Wheeler's view (in Wheeler and McLeod 1995: 286) that:

A little skill goes a long way or can be quite harmful, depending on the circumstances, and I fear that many so called person-centred counsellors have never fully embraced the full depth of theory and skill involved in competent and effective use of the model, nor embraced the full complexity of human problems they seek to treat.

This is a criticism of some people who adopt the person-centred label rather than of the approach and it is something which greatly worries person-centred practitioners who *are* conversant with theory. While the successful practice of person-centred therapy may depend upon the suspension of theoretical knowledge in the actual encounter, it must nevertheless be grounded in a thorough understanding of person-centred concepts. As I suggested in Chapter 1, perhaps the fault here lies with training courses which, although they draw on some person-centred ideas (especially the 'core conditions' as necessary to successful practice), do not really provide the grounding in the approach which, for example, the World Association for Person-Centered and Experiential Psychotherapy and Counseling, or the British Association for the Person-Centred Approach (BAPCA), would see as necessary for anyone to describe themselves as a person-centred practitioner. Graduates of these courses (which often emphasise skills and are lacking in theory) are perhaps misled into believing they have studied the person-centred approach but often have only a hazy notion of what it is. To base a criticism of the approach on the behaviours and practices of poorly trained practitioners is misguided.

Although I strongly hold to the principle I have outlined above, my experience is that the more familiar I have become with the person-centred approach, and the more immersed in it I am, the more helpful I find it to interpret *my* experience in terms of theory and to think theoretically about the human condition. I emphasise *my* experience because even when I think about another, it is only my subjective understanding to which I have access. I have found it useful to think deeply about, for example, unconditional positive regard or the nature of power, and the result of my thinking has been added clarity and changes to my practice (usually by evolution rather than revolution), *but* I am quite clear that the place for theorising is during reflection, *not* in the act of relating. This has implications for the process of assessment, diagnosis and treatment.

Person-Centred Therapy and 'Assessment'

It is probably true that many person-centred practitioners would deny that they 'assess' their clients and assert that to do so is unnecessary, even incompatible with the approach. As I indicated above, to some therapists of other orientations, this reeks of irresponsibility. Person-centred therapists do not regard themselves as lacking in a proper respect for their clients, so how do they justify their attitude to assessment? For person-centred therapists, the great problem is in the assumption that assessment is something therapists do *to* clients. That the therapist (from a position of lofty expertise) reaches some conclusion about the client's needs, and decides how therapy should proceed and for how long it may need to last, is a theoretical absurdity – perhaps it is even anathema. Even if this is an extreme view of the nature and purpose of assessment, it is something of this flavour which raises the hackles of person-centred therapists when the word is mentioned. But why, and is it the whole story? Moreover, McMahon (2000: 102–3) doubts that it is possible for a therapist *not* to assess clients. She writes:

> Even when a psychotherapist's therapeutic approach does not include assessment in a formal sense it would be difficult to avoid some form of subjective evaluation or internal assessment of the client and her needs. The evaluation of situations and people is a process learned from an early age as a necessary survival technique. Training may reduce the negative effects of such judgements, but whether it is ever possible to be totally judgement-free and 'with' the client in a completely accepting spiritual meld is more debatable.

If McMahon is right, how do person-centred therapists make sense of the inevitability of such judgements?

With respect to assessment, Mearns (1997: 91) writes:

> The whole question of client 'assessment' runs entirely counter to person-centred theory and fits those approaches to counselling which more closely align to the diagnostic 'medical model'. Within the person-centred domain the question of assessment is ridiculous: the assessor would have to make a judgement not only about the client but on the relational dimensions between the client and the counsellor.

If by 'assessment' is meant a process of diagnosis and the planning of a treatment programme, then Mearns is of course correct both in terms of person-centred theory and the way in which most person-centred practitioners understand their practice. However, there are other views, particularly from therapists who see themselves as person-centred but within the experiential tradition. Rennie (1998: 35), for example, writes of 'the need for person-centred assessment', and Speierer (1990, 1996) has developed a model which in his view allows therapy to be tailored to the individual and which explains psychological disorders of all kinds in terms of person-centred theory.

Very much in the person-centred mainstream, Bozarth (1998: 126–8) explores 'assessment via diagnosis' and, while stating that 'psychological assessment as generally conceived is incongruent with the basic assumptions of client-centered theory' (p. 127), explains where, when and under what conditions 'assessment' may be legitimate and helpful in person-centred therapy.

An alternative view of assessment would be as a process by which therapist and client come to a mutual agreement that they can work together in a beneficial way. For example, if I were to reach an understanding that I would not be able to offer a potential client one or more of Rogers' conditions, then it would be an ethical and professional obligation to refuse the contract. To do this, I must make an assessment. And, when I reflect on my own practice, I realise that, in the initial stages of a (potential) therapeutic relationship – perhaps at 'first contact', maybe in the first session, certainly in the first few – I am deciding upon the likelihood that I will be able to offer the therapist conditions to my client. This is not a structured, deliberate process – perhaps it is scarcely conscious, only becoming so when I experience myself as in some way challenged, or on reflection in supervision. Then I have more actively to decide if I am an appropriate therapist for the potential client. I can only reach this decision by examining myself – any limitation is within me, not the client. It may be that there is something in my client which arouses things within me with which I cannot immediately deal, nor can I set them on one side. In this event, I am obliged to assess *myself* as an unfit therapist for this client. So, I accept the inevitability of 'subjective evaluation' but my *intent* is to form a judgement about myself in the light of that evaluation, not about the other. It is the *attitude* and the *intent* of the counsellor *and how those are perceived by the client* that primarily distinguishes person-centred therapy. Brodley (1987: 5) characterises this person-centred attitude as

an inner experience of freedom from *assuming* what might be good or helpful for clients. It also includes being free of impulses to express one's helping instinct in the form of giving direction or interpretations. This involves an acceptance of the outsider's ignorance and helplessness in finding and effecting solutions to other people's problems. It involves, I think, a quality of humility.

Cohen (1994: 1) points out that criteria of intent define the person-centred approach, and goes on to write that person-centred practitioners

must consider not only their own intent, but the client's perception of that intent – since the phenomenological world of the client is the reality within the therapeutic relationship that is more central than is the phenomenological world of the therapist.

The issue of intent is, therefore, central to 'assessment'. I do not think that person-centred therapists would struggle anything like as much with this view. Also, my understanding from colleagues of other orientations is that, for them, this is closer to what 'assessment' actually is – that is, more of an opportunity to explore the feasibility of a counselling relationship than to impose the diagnosis of the counsellor on the client! Current research (Martin Gill, personal communication 1998) indicates that, in a British health service setting and in the initial stages of the therapeutic relationship, therapists who describe themselves as person-centred operate in essentially similar ways to those who describe themselves as psychodynamic. Gill says that the language used to describe what is happening differs but the process is the same. It may be that these supposedly different attitudes to assessment are far closer to each other than is commonly supposed.

5
Self-Actualisation: A Culture-Bound, Naive and Optimistic View of Human Nature?

There are many critics of what is assumed to be the naive optimism of person-centred practitioners. Quinn (1993: 21) considers that:

> By choosing to place an absolute and unwavering faith in the efficacy of two ultimately unprovable human dimensions (the actualising tendency and organismic valuing process), [the person-centred approach] opens itself to charges of Pollyannish optimism and therapeutic passivity.

Similarly, van Deurzen-Smith (1988: 56) criticises the assumption in humanistic psychology (and by implication person-centred therapy) that human beings are 'basically positive creatures who develop constructively, given the right conditions', and Yalom (1980: 19) questions the 'almost exclusive' emphasis on individual freedom, choice and liberation he sees as inherent to humanistic approaches. Central to this criticism is the person-centred belief that people are positively driven towards constructive growth by the actualising tendency and (mistakenly) that there is, in person-centred philosophy, an ideal endpoint to growth, the state of self-actualisation or being 'fully functioning'. This is seen as unrealistic – there is so much evidence of man's inhumanity to man that belief in the progressive nature of people is almost delusional! And so many people are manifestly not operating optimally that the belief we can do so must be mistaken. As long ago as 1959, Rogers (in Kirschenbaum and Henderson, 1990b: 27) was aware of this, but refuted the criticism:

> The emphasis on the self-directive capacity of the individual and the release of this potential through a suitable growth-promoting climate have for some reason stirred much criticism. Some have thought of the client-centered therapist as an optimist. Others have felt that this line of thought follows Rousseau. Neither criticism seems to me to be true. The hypothesis in regard to the capacity of the individual is, rather, distilled out of an accumulated experience with many mildly

and deeply disturbed individuals, who often display destructive or self-destructive tendencies. Contrary to those therapists who see depravity at men's core, who see men's deepest instincts as destructive, I have found that when man is truly free to become what he most deeply is, free to actualize his nature as an organism capable of awareness, then he clearly appears to move toward wholeness and integration.

Rogers is clear that his belief in the actualising tendency is based in empirical observation but perhaps this does not completely answer the charge of naive optimism, especially when the accusation is broadened to assert that the values of the person-centred approach are the product of midwestern, middle-class, mid-twentieth-century American thinking – that is, it reflects the values of the culture into which Rogers was born and therefore may have no relevance to cultures rooted in other times and places. Of course, person-centred practitioners take a different view. Bozarth (1998: 21–3) considers the 'myth' that 'the person-centered approach is grounded in U.S. American culture and philosophy'. This is not an argument with which he has any sympathy. He writes (p. 21):

> The position is often taken that Rogers' values were initially middle class American values and out of the US culture of valuing independence, individual resourcefulness and materialistic accomplishments. I consider this a flawed argument that fails to consider the essence of the theory as an organismic, natural and universal theory.

He also points out (p. 22) that Rogers' observations are the foundation of his theory and that these observations were of work with individuals from all over the world. The implications of the cultural origins and relevance of person-centred theory were discussed in Chapter 3. However, to attack a belief in the actualising tendency is to strike at the heart of person-centred therapy for, as Sanders (2000) points out, it is the defining characteristic of the approach. A defence of the actualising tendency is therefore paramount.

Self-Actualisation, the Fully Functioning Person and the Actualising Tendency – One and the Same?

As indicated above, there are many criticisms of 'self-actualisation' (a term which, in person-centred theory, is different from the concept of Maslow in that it is not the peak state resulting from the satisfaction of a 'hierarchy of needs'), and the concept of the 'fully functioning person' as an overly optimistic view of human nature. These are assumed to be ideal states and the goal of human development (and therefore of therapy). Williams and Irving (1996: 167) argue that, if person-centred theory were true, 'self-actualisation would be the norm, and failure to reach our full human potential would be rare'. There is a fundamental misconception here. In person-centred terms, self-actualisation is a process, not a state, and it applies only to that part of the person delineated as the 'self'; that is, a subsystem of the whole person usually called the self-concept and which Mearns and Thorne (1988: 6) define as 'the person's conceptual construction of himself'. Rogers (1959: 196) refers to the 'general tendency toward actualization' of 'that portion of the experience of the organism which is symbolized in the self', but does not imply here or elsewhere that 'self-actualisation' could, should or would result in anyone reaching their 'full human potential'. Bozarth (1998: 30) puts it thus: 'the concept defined as "Self-Actualization" is a construct referring to the actualization tendency manifest in the "self" – a subsystem that becomes differentiated within the whole person'. Self-actualisation is not a goal of either therapy or normal, healthy living. Merry (2000: 349) in his neat and succinct encapsulation of the basic assumptions of person-centred therapy, writes:

> Self-actualization, subsumed under the actualizing tendency, appears after the development of the self-concept and acts to maintain that concept. Self-actualization does not always result in optimal functioning because each person, whether psychologically healthy or unhealthy, is self-actualizing to the extent that each has a self-structure to maintain.

Furthermore, the process of self-actualisation may conflict with the actualising tendency (see Rogers 1959: 196–7; Bozarth 1998: 30; Hawtin and Moore 1998: 92). This possibility alone indicates that, in terms of person-centred theory, self-actualisation is relatively unimportant because the aim of therapy is to facilitate the congruence of the self-concept and the organism.

Arguments as to the nature of the 'fully functioning person' are essentially similar, for while this too may be taken as indicating a person-centred belief in some ideal state, it does not. In defining the 'good life' (that is, being fully functioning) Rogers (1967: 186) writes: 'it is not, in my estimation, a state of virtue, or contentment, or nirvana, or happiness. It is not a condition in which the individual is adjusted, or fulfilled, or actualized.' Like self-actualisation, the notion of the fully functioning person refers to a directional development, not a state of being. In describing the 'process of functioning more fully', Rogers (1967: 191–2) wrote of the person who is 'psychologically free':

He is more able to experience all of his feelings, and is less afraid of any of his feelings; he is his own sifter of evidence, and is more open to evidence from all sources; he is completely engaged in the process of being and becoming himself, and thus discovers that he is soundly and realistically social; he lives more completely in this moment, but learns that this is the soundest living for all time. He is becoming a more fully functioning organism, and because of the awareness of himself which flows freely in and through his experience, he is becoming a more fully functioning person.

The emphasis is clearly on a process of 'becoming'.

So, what is important in classic person-centred theory is the *actualising tendency*, a movement towards the fulfilment of potential, not 'self-actualisation' (which Rogers mentioned scarcely at all) as some ideal or personally perfect state. Of this tendency, Rogers (1951: 487) wrote that the human species 'has one basic tendency and striving – to actualize, maintain, and enhance the experiencing organism'. He clarified this statement in his classic paper of 1959, writing that the actualising tendency

involves development toward the differentiation of organs and functions, expansion in terms of growth, expansion of effectiveness through the use of tools, expansion and enhancement through reproduction. It is development toward autonomy and away from heteronomy, or control by external forces. (p. 196)

Barrett-Lennard (1998: 75) refers to a paper of Rogers published in 1963 ('The actualizing tendency in relation to "motives" and to consciousness') as 'the most systematic and complete expression of [Rogers'] thought on this topic', writing:

A central idea is that an inherent and active directional tendency is present generally in complex organic life forms, implicit even in the DNA molecule. It takes only a tolerant environment and essential nutrients for each organism to hasten on its developmental path, pushed by imperatives of its species, guided by its individual code, drawn by its own unique experience and, in the case of humans, moving also by the intentionality of evolving consciousness and meaning.

In other words, the actualising tendency is a *biological* force, common to all living things, not unique to human beings. As discussed in Chapter 3, Mearns and Thorne (2000: 177–86) offer a dialogical theory of the self in which the actualising tendency is moderated by a force of social mediation.

The actualising tendency is postulated as subsumed in a directional tendency in the universe. Of this *formative tendency* Rogers (1980: 134) wrote:

We are tapping into a tendency which permeates all of organic life – a tendency to become all the complexity of which the organism is capable. And on an even larger scale, I believe we are tuning in to a potent creative tendency which has formed our universe, from the smallest snowflake to the largest galaxy, from the lowly amoeba to the most sensitive and gifted of persons. And perhaps we are touching the cutting edge of our ability to transcend ourselves, to create new and more spiritual directions in human evolution. This kind of formulation for me is a philosophical base for the person-centred approach.

And

This is an evolutionary tendency toward greater order, greater complexity, and greater inter-relatedness. In humankind, this tendency exhibits itself as the individual moves from a single cell origin to complex organic functioning, to knowing and serving below the level of consciousness, to a conscious awareness of the organism and the external world, to a transcendent awareness of the harmony and unity of the cosmic system, including humankind. (ibid.: 139)

Perhaps the formative tendency can be understood in mystical or metaphysical terms, but for Bozarth (1998: 93) there is a remarkable similarity 'to the systems theory underlying modern physics'. To reframe these theoretical principles in terms of human ideals is mistaken. Merry (2000: 348) points out that because 'the theory of actualization is a natural science theory, not a moral theory', no values are implied.

There is also conflict between the notion of the actualising tendency and the doctrine of Original Sin. Thorne (1992a: 68–9) writes:

To the Christian, reared on the doctrinal tradition of the Fall–Redemption theology originating in St. Augustine and alive and well today, it is inconceivable that anyone could be so wilfully obtuse as to regard human nature as essentially good and forward moving; such a perception of humanity is dangerous for it suggests that men and women have no need of redemption, that they do not require a saviour and that the death and resurrection of Christ are without meaning or significance. For such Christian critics Rogers' view of human nature strikes at the very heart of their understanding of the Christian gospel and, as such, ranks as a major heresy to be eradicated at the earliest opportunity.

In 'Person-centred therapy: the path to holiness', Thorne (1996: 107–16) expresses an alternative view that 'person-centred therapy [is] a spiritual discipline with its roots firmly in the Western, Christian tradition and the Trinitarian doctrine of God as relationship' (p. 107).

The Cultural Relevance of Person-Centred Therapy

We are each products of a complexity of cultural influences. These include ethnicity and nationality, religion, class, gender and sexual orientation. Rogers and his early collaborators were, for the most part, well-educated, middle-class, white American men. It is widely believed that the theories and practices which they generated reflect their way of being in the world, are products of their culture. This being so, the argument runs, then just as its originators were confined and constrained by their culture, so must person-centred theory be. Spinelli (1989: 159) propounds this belief, writing: 'much of humanistic psychology appears to be largely culture-bound to the North American experience'. Spinelli is not alone in voicing this view, although why it should invalidate humanistic psychology any more than (for example) psychoanalysis as the product of late nineteenth-/early twentieth-century Vienna, or the whole of the Judaeo/Christian tradition as rooted in the Biblical lands of more than 2,000 years ago, is a puzzle. But then of course there are those who make precisely these arguments. If Spinelli is right, the actualising tendency and other theoretical precepts of the person-centred approach are artefacts of a particular time, place and culture and their relevance to any other time, place and culture is at least questionable. Bozarth (1998: 21–2) considers this to be a flawed argument because it ignores 'the essence of the theory as an organismic, natural and universal theory'. While I am persuaded that there is nothing culturally limiting in person-centred theory, I do see that person-centred practitioners are likely to be 'culture-bound' – for example, I *am* white, male, middle-class, middle-aged, heterosexual, and each of these attributes (and any others which may be justifiably attributable) brings with it a set of values, expectations, ways of seeing and experiencing the world; they are (at least in part) how I and others define my way of being. Does this mean that my implementation of person-centred principles is 'culture-bound'? Not necessarily, because this depends on my ability to embody the therapist conditions and to trust the actualising tendency (in me and in others). The latter is facilitated by a conscious decision not to exert power over the other. Rogers (1977: 14) expressed it thus:

> The politics of the client-centered approach is a conscious renunciation and avoidance by the therapist of all control over, or decision-making for, the client. It is the facilitation of self-ownership by the

client and the strategies by which this can be achieved; the placing of a locus of decision-making and the responsibility for the effects of these decisions. It is politically centred in the client.

Owen (1990: 93), however, takes the view that 'culture clash' is inevitable in therapy:

Problems of different cultural beliefs between counsellors and clients lead to a culture clash when each party's hidden rules conflict. There is no one without prejudices based on their own cultural beliefs about morals, values, social, religious, economic, educational, political, ethnic or sexual criteria. This is particularly true in class-bound Britain. We all have culture and an upbringing. The values and beliefs we have limit us. If we did not have values or beliefs we would be indifferent to everything.

Therefore, in a sense, all counselling is cross-cultural counselling.

Owen (p. 94) goes on to state that 'client-centred' counsellors will work more effectively if they take on board their client's differences and adjust their style accordingly. He recommends a reading of the medical anthropology literature as a way of doing this.

To assume that any theory can belong wholly to one time and place may be mistaken. Maybe it is equally valid to view the development of human thought as a process through which it is possible to trace connections, inspirations and diversions rather than as a series of fixed points? For example, Hendrik de Vos speaking at the Person-Centered Forum in Johannesburg, 1998, traced the 'maieutic' quality of dialogue from Socrates, through Kierkegaard to Rogers, seeing 'non-directivity' as essentially Socratic. Of course the first expression or statement of a new contribution will be coloured by the times and experiences of its author but no thought springs unparented into the world. Perhaps the optimism of mid-twentieth-century, middle America and a cultural emphasis on rugged individualism did contribute to the development of humanistic psychology – but so did the philosophy and metaphysics of the ancient Western world, an increasing awareness of Eastern thought and so on. And why assume that humanistic psychology ceased to develop and change after the early declarations of Maslow and Rogers, among others? Is it not equally possible that as these ideas were encountered by people of other times and cultures they were adapted, transformed and fed back into the mainstream, so moderating and modifying theory and practice? If not, why is it possible for a young British Moslem woman of Pakistani origin deeply immersed in her culture to believe that the person-centred approach is of relevance to her life (personal communication 1998)? Why for that matter should it make sense to me, a Briton, some 40 or so years younger than the progenitors of humanistic psychology? And yet it does. And how can Morotomi (1998: 28–32) write of the compatibility of person-centred theory and Japanese spirituality? Indeed he writes (p. 28) of the reason for the popularity of the person-centred approach in Japan: 'it has something to do with the similarity between Rogers' view of life and nature and the one that permeates the lives of ordinary Japanese people'. Kuno (2001: 210–19) seemingly agrees with this, showing the agreement between the concept of unconditional positive regard and the Buddhist beliefs and practices deeply embedded in Japanese culture. Similarly, many people who attended the Person-Centred Forum in Johannesburg, 1998, were from African cultures. It was apparent that they saw no contradiction between their traditional way of viewing the world and their understanding of the person-centred approach. As with Morotomi's and Kuno's interpretations of person-centred theory in terms of their culture, Zulu members of this gathering pointed out the essential similarity between person-centred concepts and the practice of their 'folk medicine' and, in particular, the concept of 'uBuntu', which is the Zulu word for 'humanness'.

The person-centred approach can also be understood from a variety of religious and mystical perspectives. Purton (1996: 455–67) explores the significant parallels between views of the person, and of therapy, in Buddhism and in the work of Carl Rogers and, with respect to Soto Zen, Moore (2001: 207–8) writes of a similar accord. Hermsen (1996: 107–25) deals with the similarity between the person-centred approach and Taoism; Thorne (1996: 107–16) 'explicitly defines person-centred therapy as a spiritual discipline with its roots firmly in the Western, Christian tradition', and in one of his books (1991) emphasises the 'spiritual dimensions' of person-centred counselling; MacMillan (1999: 47–61) is struck by the parallels between the work of a Sufi mystic and the person-centred approach; and Cameron (1999: 101–6) finds person-centred theory provides a framework to support her understanding of 'subtle energy exchanges in the counselling relationship'.

While there is a theoretical response to the charge that person-centred theory is limited, I think it is at least equally persuasive that people so culturally diverse can find something of meaning in it – this throws doubt on the idea that person-centred therapy is culture-bound. I will say too that as I have listened to these understandings and interpretations of the approach, my own understanding of it has been expanded.

The Transcultural Dimension

Bimrose (2000: 26–8) has pointed out that 'social contexts' can be overlooked in counselling because of the preoccupation with the individual client. She considers that 'reconciling the focus on the individual client with … an understanding of their socio-cultural contexts has become an important issue within the broad areas of counselling and therapy' (p. 27). Owen (1996: 187–94) considers 'the person-centred approach in a cultural context', arguing that 'all counselling is cross-cultural' and that this has implications for person-centred practice. He states (pp. 192–3):

> If person-centred therapy has the aim of providing appropriate care for each client, then this care is appropriate according to the individual's personality, cultural group, educational, moral, political, sexual, family, religious and other relevant considerations…counsellors need to design a therapeutic structure in which each case takes into account the individuality and cultural context of each client….Person-centred counsellors need to be culturally sensitive in the service of clients.

'Cultural awareness' has been an issue for person-centred practitioners from the earliest days. Writing of 'transcultural counselling', d'Ardenne and Mahtani (1989: 1–2) record that while some counselling theorists appear to believe that 'good counsellors' (that is, those who are warm, genuine and understanding) are effective 'with all their clients, whether within or between cultures', Rogers believed that it was important that therapists had some knowledge of their client's cultural setting. Indeed, Rogers wrote (1951: 437):

> Such knowledge needs to be supplemented by experiences of living or dealing with individuals who have been the product of cultural influences very different from those which have molded (the counsellor).

However, d'Ardenne and Mahtani (1989: 2) do consider that Rogers did not examine and explain the concept of 'culture', neither did he indicate the skills necessary to work with someone from a different cultural background. Just what issues may arise from cultural differences and how they are relevant to counselling are dealt with (at least to some extent) in Feltham and Horton (2000: 28–70), where various authors consider issues of gender, disability, age, social class, sexual orientation, religion and secular assumptions, race, culture and ethnicity. Although they may consider particular theoretical and practical approaches (for example, Mohamed 2000: 66–9 discusses transcultural therapy), there is often an emphasis on seeing people for who they are, that is, acknowledging that a client is black or gay, for example, and that is relevant, but not acting on the assumption that this is *all* they are – and never assuming that the 'problem' lies in the difference. Davies (2000: 54–5) could be writing about any minority group when he states:

> Don't assume that clients' sexual orientation is the cause of their difficulties. Lesbian, gay and bisexual people may present for counselling or therapy with a range of life issues (relationship breakdown, bereavement, anxiety, depression, work stress, etc.). Most of these issues bear little direct relevance to their sexuality, although often coloured by the experience of being a sexual minority in an oppressive and discriminatory society.

There is also a widespread tendency to emphasise the responsibility of therapists to address their own relevant issues. Thorne (2000: 61) writes: 'counsellors who wish to work effectively with those experiencing religious or spiritual concerns need to accept the stern discipline of pursuing their own spiritual journey with unflagging commitment'. Mohamed (2000: 67) combines these two elements when she writes: 'a white therapist may consciously see a black client rather than the person they are. If they have not examined the way that they stereotype and make judgements, they may deny what they have projected into blackness.' My current position is that since the person-centred approach requires me to respond to others as and who they are, to trust that they will 'develop' in a way which is right for them, it is incumbent upon me to address anything and everything which may get in the way of so doing. This seems to be what is required when working with 'difference', and implies that in some way, when properly conducted, person-centred therapy is 'culture free': Bozarth's contention of universality of the theory seems to hold true. But does this mean that person-centred therapy is appropriate in any social context? Pilgrim (2000: 49), writing about social class, states that, in his experience, 'a problem-solving approach, rather than one which is either rigidly non-directive (attending *only* to the purported necessary and sufficient conditions of the central therapeutic triad) or psychodynamic' is one with which clients of the British National Health Service can engage and from which they can profit. For Pilgrim, this true whatever the social class of the client, 'but especially those from a poor background'. Of course, this may say more about Pilgrim and his clients than it does about any approach to therapy, but the fact remains that his findings indicate that person-centred therapy is not effective. Kearney (1997: 11) implies that it is not person-centred therapy *per se* which is inappropriate to working with issues of class but a 'dilution of former ideals in counselling'. She writes: 'Interpretations of Rogerian counselling which emphasise the individual as distinct from "the individual in her/his social context" have gained precedence over readings of Rogers' work which charge the counsellor with a social as well as a personal responsibility to clients', and considers that 'the class basis of counselling and the power issues surrounding class remain, for the most part, obscured and ignored' (p. 12). This is also part of Pilgrim's argument. There is no reason to suppose that person-centred practitioners are any better (or worse) at 'class awareness' than therapists of any other stripe. But, again, this does not necessarily reflect an inherent weakness in the theory but in its implementation and the training of person-centred practitioners.

Are People Good, Bad or Indifferent?

There is a widely held view that person-centred theory holds that people are 'essentially good' – a view with which many person-centred practitioners would perhaps agree. This presumed assumption of inherent goodness is doubted by some. It apparently conflicts with observations of human behaviour over the centuries (the Nazi holocaust, Apartheid and the killing fields of Cambodia, to name but a few examples from the twentieth century) and is contested by other theories and some religious doctrine. There is a debate between Rogers and Rollo May (whom Rogers described as a leading scholar of humanistic psychology) which addresses this – see Kirschenbaum and Henderson (1990b: 239–55). Rogers (pp. 237–8) writes that May 'sees the demonic as a basic element in the human makeup' but that he (Rogers), although 'very well aware of the incredible amount of destructive, cruel, malevolent behaviour in today's world', does not find that people are inherently evil. May's response points out (p. 240) that his term is *daimonic* which is different from 'demonic' and means 'the urge in every being to affirm itself, assert itself, perpetuate and increase itself'. This drive is the source of both constructive and destructive impulses. May clearly believes that people have the potential for both good and evil and that 'the issue of evil- or rather, not confronting evil – has profound, and to my mind adverse effects on humanistic psychology' (p. 249). He also expresses the fear 'that if we ignore evil, we will move closer to doom, and the growth and triumph of evil may well result' (p. 250).

Thorne (1992a: 66–8) explores the conflict between the view Rogers took of human nature and the Freudian and behavioural positions. Describing what he views as Freud's 'pessimistic' view of human nature, Thorne (1992a: 66–7) goes on:

Many analytical theorists regard Rogers' view of human nature not only as naive but also as seriously misguided because it fails to do justice to the unconscious which, for the analytical practitioner, largely determines an individual's behaviour and perception of reality.

Wheeler (in Wheeler and McLeod 1995: 286) expresses this well:

A serious reservation I have about person-centred counselling is the belief in humanity as inherently good. In my experience, Freud's concepts of Eros and Thanatos, the life and death instincts and Klein's defence mechanism of splitting into good and bad, love and hate, are fundamental to all relationships, including the counselling relationship.

But is the 'inherent goodness' of people part of person-centred theory? The concept is not mentioned in the classic statements of theories of personality, the fully functioning person and inter-relationships in Rogers (1959) nor in 'A note on the nature of man' (see Kirschenbaum and Henderson 1990a: 401–8). In the latter, Rogers (p. 403) considers 'what man is *not*', stating:

I do not discover man to be well characterized in his basic nature by such terms as *fundamentally hostile, antisocial, destructive, evil.*

I do not discover man to be, in his basic nature, completely without a nature, a tabula rasa on which *anything* may be written, nor malleable putty which can be shaped into *any* form.

I do not discover man to be essentially a perfect being, sadly warped and corrupted by society.

In my experience I have discovered man to have characteristics which seem inherent in his species, and the terms which have at different times seemed to me descriptive of these characteristics are such terms as *positive, forward-moving, constructive, realistic, trustworthy.*

So (unless that which is not 'evil' is 'good'), Rogers did not here define people as good, and actually states that people are not perfect. His partial description of the nature of people is essentially biological – a statement of what (in Rogers' opinion) 'is', rather than a value judgement. Why then has this notion of 'goodness' been attached to person-centred theory? Perhaps it has something to do with the many meanings which the word 'good' carries. My spell-checker has just given me 90 synonyms for it, grouped in 14 categories. How can this but lead to ambiguity? However, of these 90 synonyms, the only word also in Rogers' list is 'trustworthy'. It seems clear that the attribution comes from outside the approach and results from imposing an understanding of (for example) 'constructive' as having moral value, being 'good', when what is meant is growing, becoming more complex. Also, it is a statement of fact arising from empirical observation, not a declaration of a desirable or admirable quality. It is the same mistake as interpreting the Darwinian notion of 'survival of the fittest' as meaning that the 'best' or the 'strongest' will survive, when what is meant is 'the best shaped', that is the most suited to take advantage of a particular niche. Both are statements about biology, neither implies a moral judgement, and both have the status of theory derived from observation, not that of proven 'fact'. Arguments about 'inherent goodness' are spurious – it is neither stated nor implied. People are of worth, they are constructive, they are trustworthy – this does not mean that they are inherently and innately saintly!

Wheeler's principal concern is that what she sees as the person-centred position with respect to 'inherent goodness' leads to an avoidance of 'thoughts and feelings such as envy, murderous rage, bitterness and hatred'. Of course person-centred practitioners know that these are real emotions experienced by most people at some time in their lives – to feel 'murderous', spiteful or sadistic does not alter one's status as of inherent worth. Not only do we know about them but we encounter them in our clients, in our selves and in others. Sometimes in the process of person-centred therapy, they are directed towards the counsellor. From a theoretical point of view, it is the six conditions (perhaps especially unconditional positive regard) which allow their expression. Rogers (1967: 177, for example) and other person-centred writers make so many references to the expression of 'negative' emotions that I find it difficult to understand how this particular myth has arisen. In my own practice I have encountered clients who have expressed virulent hatred for another, wishing them dead, I have experienced frustration and anger directed towards me for things I am perceived to have done and for things I 'should' have done, and I have heard descriptions of acts of which the teller was deeply ashamed. Envy and jealousy too have been present in my therapeutic relationships – in fact the whole gamut of human emotions. I know from acting as a supervisor for other person-centred therapists that they too encounter feelings of every kind. In addition, there is no reason why the therapist cannot mention such powerful feelings first, perhaps as the result of an empathic sensing, however tentative, perhaps as necessary to maintaining congruence. Nor is 'confrontation' impossible in person-centred therapy. Lietaer (1984: 54–7) discusses 'confrontation and unconditionality' and points out that 'confrontation does not in any way mean that I reject my client as a person or that I stop trying to understand his experience' (p. 56). If the unconditional positive regard of the therapist is experienced by the client, then challenge and confrontation may play a useful part in therapy – certainly, being person-centred is not about being passive or 'nice' – but a necessary component of unconditional positive regard is an acceptance of the client's authority and self-expertise. So, it is possible to act in a challenging or confrontational way and still be person-centred. Kilborn (1999: 37–46) conducted a small survey of person-centred therapists, asking them about the role of 'challenge' in person-centred theory and practice. Her informants reported that 'challenge had an important place in the person-centred approach', that 'the core conditions, by their very nature, constituted a challenge to the client' and that, in the context of a trusting relationship, challenge 'becomes an integral part of the therapy and flows from it'. She also describes how one of her informants saw 'pure, loving anger, congruently expressed' as providing a challenge to the client 'which is nearly always productive', and offers this illustrative quotation: 'I feel myself enraged at the power within you that threatens to keep you from the truth that you are loveable and loved.' This may indeed be a challenge, it may be based in congruence but, most importantly, it is deeply accepting. Actually, in unconditional positive regard (or rather what I increasingly see as a condition which is a fusion of that and empathy), person-centred therapists have a powerful tool for aiding clients to contact and express powerful, negative and shameful feelings. When in tune, they are able to convey to the client something like: 'I know you feel murderous, I can even feel it within me – that does not change my sense of you as a person of worth.' Theory and experience teach me that this can lead to an even deeper connection with destructive impulses, negative and shameful emotions, bitterness and the like. It is when this connection is deeply felt and openly expressed that change of some kind is likely to occur.

6
The Core Conditions: Necessary but Insufficient?

Are There 'Core' Conditions?

One of the most widespread misunderstandings about person-centred theory is the assumption that, according to it, there are three 'core conditions' the demonstration of which is all that is needed for successful therapy. This is not so. Rogers (1957: 95–103) listed six conditions which he thought were *necessary* and *sufficient* for therapeutic change. These were essential to *any* successful therapy – that is, Rogers was making an integrative statement. He states that, if these conditions are present, positive change *will* occur *regardless* of the orientation of the practitioner – 'whether we are thinking of classical psychoanalysis, or any of its modern offshoots, or Adlerian psychotherapy, or any other' (Rogers 1957: 101). As set out in 1957 (p. 96) these conditions are:

1. Two persons are in psychological contact.
2. The first, whom we shall term the client, is in a state of incongruence, being vulnerable or anxious.
3. The second person, whom we shall term the therapist, is congruent or integrated in the relationship.
4. The therapist experiences unconditional positive regard for the client.
5. The therapist experiences an empathic understanding of the client's internal frame of reference and endeavours to communicate this experience to the client.
6. The communication to the client of the therapist's empathic understanding and unconditional positive regard is to a minimal degree achieved.

Conditions 3, 4 and 5 are sometimes referred to as the 'core conditions' of congruence, unconditional positive regard (or acceptance) and empathy. In Rogers' paper (1959: 213) which is taken to be a statement of the principles of the person-centred approach, these conditions are stated slightly differently:

1. That two persons are in *contact*.
2. That the first person, whom we shall term the client, is in a state of *incongruence*, being *vulnerable*, or *anxious*.

3. That the second person, whom we shall term the therapist, is *congruent* in the *relationship*.
4. That the therapist is *experiencing unconditional positive regard* toward the client.
5. That the therapist is *experiencing* an *empathic* understanding of the client's *internal frame of reference*.
6. That the client *perceives*, at least to a minimal degree, conditions 4 and 5, the *unconditional positive regard* of the therapist for him, and the *empathic* understanding of the therapist.

It is often assumed that the 1959 statement in some way represents a refinement of the 1957 statement but, as Bozarth (1998: 104) states:

It is difficult to determine whether or not these subtle differences have any meaning; however, it seems unlikely that Rogers would be cavalier with statements that were incorporated in what he considered the most rigorous expositions of his belief and of his theory.

However, Tudor and Merry (2002: 24) report that the 1959 chapter was written *before* the 1957 paper. For them, the fact that the later publication actually takes historical precedence resolves some of the debates. They state:

although *published* [in 1959] two years after the 1957 paper [the 1959 chapter] was actually written and completed between 1953 and 1955 *before* the 1957 paper (which was received for publication in 1956) ... the delay [being] due to the scale of Sigmund Koch's enterprise in editing a series of volumes on *Psychology: A Study of a Science* and the timescale of publication. Over the years there has been some considerable debate as to the significance of differences in the two statements, especially regarding the term CONTACT (1959 chapter) and PSYCHOLOGICAL CONTACT (1957 paper) and the necessity (or otherwise) of the therapist's *communication* of their unconditional positive regard and empathic understanding to the client (1957) or the sufficiency that these attitudes are *perceived* (1959). Considerable light is shed on such debates by the clarification that the more comprehensive formulation takes historical precedence and that the papers were written with different purposes in mind.

What this does not alter is that the 1957 paper is a statement about any successful therapy (although Rogers (1957: 101), explicitly states that psychotherapy is *not* a special kind of relationship—the conditions can be and are met in many others), and the 1959 paper is specifically about 'client-centered' therapy.

The assumption that there are 'core' conditions has led to people acting, writing and thinking as if it is only these which matter. Presumably, Rogers (who rarely if ever used this term himself) implied no ranking of the six conditions – it is in combination that they are necessary and sufficient. Exclude any, and the proposition falls. However, he (see, for example, Kirschenbaum and Henderson 1990a: 135) did speak of 'three conditions which constitute [a] growth-promoting climate', meaning those attributes referred to as the core conditions. These Rogers states are characteristic of *any* situation in which the development of the person is a goal. In a way, conditions 1 and 2 (the requirement for contact and the requirement that the person in the client role be incongruent) can be viewed as necessary pre-conditions for therapy but this does not alter the need for their presence.

Tudor (2000: 33–7) discusses the 'lost conditions', stressing that it is not the 'core conditions' which are necessary and sufficient but all six. He (p. 34) considers that emphasis on the 'core' conditions leads to:

> the theoretical denial and distortion of the central hypothesis of the [person-centred approach] and specifically the nature of therapeutic and helping relationships, perpetuates a reduced version of the approach and confirms a limited and insufficient view of person-centred theory and therapy.

He goes on to state (p. 35) that there are four principal problems arising from the notion of 'core' conditions. These are:

> The view that the 'core conditions' are necessary and sufficient.
> The view that, by naming them together, they are the same in nature.
> The view that they are, in some way, 'core' or at the heart of this theory – and indeed the [person-centred approach].
> The corollary – that the other three conditions are less 'core' or central.

This is of great importance when any evaluation of person-centred therapy is attempted – unfortunately many researchers concentrate on the core conditions either together or severally – the latter making even less sense. Research into empathy, unconditional positive regard and/or congruence may allow the researchers to draw conclusions about these qualities separately or in combination but it is not a test of Rogers' hypothesis of the necessity and sufficiency of the *six* conditions. Hargie and Gallagher (1992: 153–7), for example, present a 'comparison of the core conditions of client-centred counselling in real and role-play counselling episodes'. In their introduction (p. 153) they state that Rogers claimed that 'empathy, acceptance and genuineness' are 'the necessary and sufficient conditions for effective counselling' – but he did not. This research, which raises some valuable points and from which the authors draw interesting conclusions, can say nothing about Rogers' hypothesis – to be fair, the authors neither state nor imply that it does but it seems that such research is often re-interpreted by others as if it did. Perhaps it can not be emphasised enough but it seems important to restate that:

Person-centred theory does not and has never asserted that the so-called 'core conditions' of empathy, unconditional positive regard and congruence are the necessary and sufficient conditions for constructive personality change to occur.

There have been studies exploring the therapeutic relationship (Patterson, 1984: 431, in his 'review of reviews' states that research on 'the core conditions of the counselling and psychotherapy relationship is voluminous'), but those which take into account all the hypothesised conditions are rare if they exist at all. This led Watson (1984: 17–40) in his review of research studies to conclude (p. 40) that 'after twenty-five years of research on Rogers' hypotheses, there is not yet research of the rigor required for drawing conclusions about the validity of this important theory'. Although Bozarth's (1998: 163–73) survey of research in psychotherapy outcome indicates that 'the most clear research evidence is that effective psychotherapy results from the resources of the client (extratherapeutic variables) and from the person-to-person relationship of the therapist and client' (pp. 172–3), it appears that 18 years after the publication of Watson's paper, it remains the case that there is a lack of research. A further statement therefore seems appropriate:

The hypothesis that the six conditions as stated by Rogers in 1957 are necessary and sufficient for constructive personality change to occur is untested by rigorous research and is therefore neither proven nor disproven.

There are, however, many studies which indicate the primacy of the relationship in the therapeutic process – this primacy being implicit in Rogers' hypothesis. Bozarth (1998: 161–73) presents an overview of research on psychotherapy outcome and the person-centred approach and provides a summary of the findings of reviews of outcome studies (p. 165). These are:

Effective psychotherapy is primarily predicated upon (a) the relationship between the therapist and the client and (b) the inner and external resources of the client.
The type of therapy and technique is largely irrelevant in terms of successful outcome.

Training, credentials and experience of therapists are irrelevant to successful therapy.
Clients who receive psychotherapy improve more than clients who do not receive psychotherapy.
There is little evidence to support the position that there are specific treatments for particular disabilities.
The most consistent of the relationship variables related to effectiveness are the conditions of empathy, genuineness and unconditional positive regard.

In these findings, there is a lot of support for Rogers' central hypothesis, but they are still short of 'proof'. However, the notion of 'proof' in this context is itself susceptible to criticism. The notions of proof and disproof are peculiar to positivistic research where the minimum criteria for research are the statement of an hypothesis and the testing of that hypothesis. This leads to the somewhat scary notion that research is done in laboratories and is the province of *men* in white coats. Rogers seems to have given up on the scientific method at a relatively early stage in his career (he was questioning logical positivism in the 1950s – see Rogers 1959: 251) because it did not seem to him to be able to provide the answers to the questions he wished to ask. He later (1985, see Kirschenbaum and Henderson 1990a: 281) argued the need for a 'new science' and, although he does not appear to have used them himself, he valued the methods described by (for example) Reason and Rowan (1981), Mearns and McLeod (1984) and Douglass and Moustakas (1985). As I state elsewhere (Wilkins 1997d: 47), as well as being in accord with the scientific or positivistic paradigm 'Research may also be hypothesis or theory generating, exploratory or explanatory. It may just as legitimately seek the expression and understanding of meaning; that is be synthetic rather than analytic.' It might very well be that the convincing evidence for the efficacy of person-centred practice required by some is to be found in the deployment of these newer, more subjective and creative approaches which address 'meaning' more than 'fact'. That is, perhaps it is more important to explore the human experience of person-centred therapy (from all perspectives) than to look for what might be a spurious 'proof' of its effectiveness. For example, how can the actualising tendency (or empathy, congruence and unconditional positive regard) be understood except via the subjective experience and understanding of those experiencing it?

Whether rightly or wrongly, it is the core conditions which have been emphasised in theory, practice and research although Merry (2000: 348) points out that the first condition (the requirement for contact/psychological contact) 'is currently receiving more attention' and so is client perception and 'communication' – that is, condition 6. However, because of the emphasis on the 'core conditions' elsewhere, it is adopted here in as much as the relationship, unconditional positive regard, empathy and congruence are considered separately.

The Question of 'Sufficiency'

Even though Patterson (1984: 437) asserts that 'the evidence for the necessity, if not the sufficiency, of the therapist conditions of accurate empathy, respect, or warmth, and therapeutic genuineness is incontrovertible', the proposition that Rogers' conditions are 'necessary and sufficient' is often dismissed by therapists of other orientations (see for example Lazarus 1993: 404–7) who may argue that while they are necessary in the forming of a therapeutic relationship, these conditions are not sufficient to engender change. Something else is needed. What this may be varies with the orientation of the doubter but it always rests in the techniques and expertise available to them and apparently eschewed by person-centred therapists. There are even arguments that the core conditions (severally or together) may be counter-therapeutic (for example, empathy may encourage a client to wallow in self-pity rather than to change). Often, while broad agreement with person-centred theory is indicated, so are reservations, refinements or differences. For example, Dryden (1990: 17–18) records that while rational-emotive behaviour therapists agree with the need for the core conditions, 'particularly the importance of unconditional acceptance and genuineness' (the latter is a synonym for congruence), he doubts the value of 'warmth'. He further points out that rational-emotive behaviour counsellors offer not only 'affective empathy' but also 'philosophic empathy'. The former is roughly akin to the person-centred concept – that is, an understanding of the client's inner world – the latter has to do with understanding 'the philosophies that underpin these feelings'. However, they are critical of offering clients 'undue counsellor warmth' (warmth is one of Rogers' synonyms for unconditional positive regard). This, Dryden goes on (p. 18), is because:

First, counsellor warmth may unwittingly reinforce clients' dire need for love and approval – an irrational belief which is believed to lie at the core of much psychological disturbance. Secondly, counsellor warmth may also reinforce the philosophy of low frustration tolerance that many clients have.

Even though Dryden acknowledges the place of the therapist conditions, he appears to be led to an almost opposite conclusion about the effect of 'warmth' from that stated in person-centred theory. As Rogers (1959: 230) points out in his section on re-integration, it is the communicated unconditional positive regard of 'a significant other' which facilitates a decrease in conditions of worth and an increase in unconditional self-regard. This must result in an increasing internalisation of the locus of evaluation and thus a decreasing need for 'approval'. From the point of view of psychosynthesis, Whitmore (1991: 22) indicates the agreement between Rogers and Assagioli as to the importance of the relationship in the therapeutic process, but her list of 'counsellor attitudes' (pp. 26–34) includes not only acceptance (which 'is similar to Rogers' concept of unconditional positive regard') but also 'knowing and understanding', 'confirming' (also used by Rogers – see Tudor and Merry 2002: 27–8), 'non-attachment to outcome', 'stimulating' and 'connecting'. Other than confirmation which Rogers (1967: 55) clearly links to the acceptance of a person 'as a process of becoming'), it is probably only non-attachment to outcome which is shared with person-centred therapists. Sometimes the same terms are used by therapists of other orientations but the meaning or understanding of the effects of a condition or attitude is different. For example, Jacobs (1988: 13) records that a psychodynamic counsellor would expect 'unconditional regard' to encourage positive transference and (p. 29) equates empathy with identification. In person-centred terms, it is the 'as if' quality which separates empathy and identification. Sometimes it appears that the same processes are differently named in different approaches. For example, I have shown (Wilkins 1997b: 38) that some empathic experiences could be understood in terms of countertransference. References to empathy and 'acceptance' are relatively common from therapists of other orientations but congruence is mentioned hardly at all.

Rogers' six conditions have also been questioned (at least in terms of what qualities should be emphasised) by some who claim allegiance to the greater person-centred community (see for example Quinn 1993: 6–23) and evaluated by others. Bozarth (1998: 165–73) re-examines the findings of research into therapist attitudes (citing seven studies) and argues that they demonstrate the effectiveness of Rogers' conditions. Although there is a widespread acceptance in the greater person-centred community that the six conditions are 'necessary and sufficient', this does not mean that person-centred practitioners are unthinking about them – they are constantly being 'reconsidered' (see, for example, Tudor and Worrall 1994; Bohart and Greenberg 1997; and Wilkins 2000a), teased apart, integrated and their 'necessity' and their 'sufficiency' constantly investigated and/or deliberated upon. Bozarth (1993: 92–105), for example, examines reviews of research, the literature and person-centred theory and states (p. 102):

There is no substantial evidence to refute Rogers' position. Further consideration of the theoretical underpinnings suggests to me that, rather than conclude the conditions are *necessary but not sufficient*, it is more accurate to conclude that the conditions are *not necessarily necessary but always sufficient*.

And Brazier (1993: 72–91) postulates that 'the necessary condition is love', arguing that it is the client's rediscovery of an innate altruism which is facilitative.

The Importance of the Relationship

Even though there may be reservations about the sufficiency of the conditions, it seems that there is an increasingly wide acceptance of the importance of the relationship between client and therapist as the agent of therapeutic efficacy. Laungani (1995: 114) states, 'it appears that the personality characteristics of the therapist – in particular, warmth, trust, and acceptance – play a crucial role in determining the positive outcome of therapy' and cites research evidence for this view. From a social constructivist perspective, in their review of research Sexton and Whiston (1994: 7) state: 'it is only the counseling relationship that has consistently been found to contribute to the success of the therapeutic process'. Similarly, in their critique of Rogers' work with Mary Jane Tilden from 'a contemporary psychoanalytic perspective', Geller and Gould (1996: 217–18) write of the importance of the therapeutic alliance – although in their view with this client Rogers fell some way short of the ideal. In addition, some elements of the interaction indicated 'an alliance in need of repair', but they do say 'we believe that if Rogers were working today, he would have monitored and clarified, in an ongoing fashion, Mary Jane's ambivalent involvement in therapy'. Although Bozarth (1998: 164) takes issue with the re-framing of 'relationship' as 'alliance' in much of the literature, what seems to be consistent is the recognition that it is something about the process between therapist and client and the way they relate which is much more important to successful outcome than the 'content' of therapy sessions or the knowledge, skills and techniques of the practitioner. I understand this to be in accord with Rogers' integrative statement of 1957 – 'It ain't what you do, it's the way that you do it.' Although there is widespread agreement as to the efficacy of the therapy relationship *per se*, there are other views – even that it is intrinsically harmful. Perhaps foremost among critics is Jeffrey Masson.

In his attack on the field of psychotherapy as a whole, Masson (1992: 229–47) devotes a whole chapter to Rogers and client-centred therapy. This chapter he entitles 'The problem with benevolence'. Masson regards all psychotherapy as oppressive, and Rogers (and therefore the person-centred approach) as benevolently despotic – but despotic nevertheless. He presents (pp. 233–6) a critique of the 'core' conditions and clearly regards unconditional positive regard and congruence in particular as impossible to guarantee – perhaps even impossible to achieve. I think that many of Masson's arguments are based on misunderstandings. This sometimes appears to arise from a slight twist in emphasis or the addition or omission of a word. For example, he writes (p. 233): 'There is no reason to believe that ... any therapist necessarily *feels* [my emphasis] "congruent" or "integrated" in relationship *to* [my emphasis] his client.' In the first place, Masson appears to assume that congruence is a feeling rather than a way of being. Secondly, the insertion of the preposition 'to' (Rogers' condition is that the therapist is congruent or integrated *in* the relationship) changes the meaning. The congruence or integration is within the therapist *while* relating to the client – there is no suggestion that the integration is somehow between the therapist and the client. Similarly, Masson (p. 234) refers to unconditional positive regard as an emotion, but it is described by Rogers and others as an attitude. Masson (p. 234) adopts the view that the ability to offer the six conditions should be constant, asking 'what guarantee could there possibly be, that any given therapist is this genuine person Rogers posits him to be?' Luckily, Rogers (1957: 97) was not as demanding as Masson assumed and acknowledges the impossibility of maintaining congruence at all times and in all areas of life. He explains just what to be congruent as a therapist might entail:

It is not necessary (nor is it possible) that the therapist be a paragon who exhibits this degree of integration, of wholeness, in every aspect of his life. It is sufficient that he is accurately himself in this hour of this relationship, that in this basic sense he is what he is, in this moment of time.

It should be clear that this includes being himself even in ways which are not regarded as ideal for psychotherapy. His experience may be 'I am afraid of this client' or 'My attention is so focused on my own problems that I can scarcely listen to him.' If the therapist is not denying these feelings to awareness, but is able freely to be them (as well as being his other feelings), then [the requirement for congruence] is met.

Clearly, Rogers and Masson have very different ideas as to what congruence means and what is required of a congruent therapist.

How Can Anyone *Guarantee* Unconditional Positive Regard?

The unconditional positive regard of the counsellor for the client is a *necessary* condition for constructive change. And yet the world is full of hostile, reprehensible, malefic individuals. How can they possibly be acceptable to anybody? Not unreasonably, and leaving aside the important matter of definition, Masson (1992: 234) asks: 'Faced with a brutal rapist who murders children, why should any therapist have unconditional regard for him?' (Masson omits 'positive'). There is no reason at all why any therapist *should* but the therapeutic endeavour will be pointless without it. I have asserted elsewhere (Wilkins 2000a) that while therapists may be limited by their ability to offer unconditional positive regard, this in no way implies that person-centred therapy is similarly limited. Theory asserts that *if* (for example) a paedophile consistently experiences the six conditions, then therapeutic change *will* occur. Of course it may be that this is a big 'if'. But what is important is that it is realised that the limitation is in the practitioner, not the theory. This does, of course, raise the question of whether, given the nature of people (not excepting counsellors and psychotherapists) as, often and at least to some extent, prejudiced, fearful beings, the theory can ever be put to the test. Luckily, although we share the tendency to be unaccepting of some things, these are not necessarily the same things and we may therefore be appropriate therapists for different clients. There are people for whom (because of my own fears and unresolved issues?) my unconditional positive regard is limited, but there are some whom others may experience great difficulty in accepting but with whom I can form an accepting relationship. Also, it is my experience that I can learn to see what (perhaps more importantly, who) lies behind 'unacceptable behaviour' – this increases my ability to offer unconditional positive regard. I see no reason to believe I am unique, or even unusual in this respect. An illustration from my own experience (adapted from Wilkins 2000a: 27–8) may help:

A 'difficult' client presented at my place of work. He had previously been seen by one of my colleagues, of whom he had little good to say. In his expressed view, the service for which we worked was useless and counselling was worse. And yet he wanted an appointment. With some foreboding, I agreed to meet with him for counselling. I had a sense of being tested to my limits. This was confirmed when he arrived for his first appointment driving an army surplus armoured car and began telling me of his love of the military and hatred of most people; women and black people in particular. All this challenged my liberal attitudes – and awakened painful memories of being badly beaten by soldiers many years before, and yet I knew that the efficacy of our relationship depended upon me being accepting, not merely acting the part.

As I listened and responded to him, I was increasingly able to separate my story from his and I began to wonder about what life experiences had led him to his extreme views. The tale he told was of mistreatment as a child and a tempestuous relationship with his wife, who he experienced as 'robbing' him of his house and his business. Between sessions, I read about prejudice and how it might arise. Almost without noticing, I slipped from being challenged by my client's way of being to an appreciation of the person of worth behind the views. As this happened, there was a softening in him, sessions began to include humour and a sense of companionship in the counselling enterprise. It was as if, as I became increasingly able to feel warm, caring and accepting towards him, he accepted himself more and became more accepting of the world.

To offer this client unconditional positive regard, I had to do two main things. One was to recognise what it was about his way of being which aroused my prejudices (for example, with respect to the military) and to deal with them. Sometimes the recognition is enough – 'Ah, that's where that is coming from!' Sometimes supervision or personal therapy is a way of resolving or setting aside such issues. The second was to 'listen' to the person. The first is a necessary precursor to the second. In this case, I remember quite suddenly having the sense that I was dealing with someone deeply wounded who was driven by pain to lash out – and it seemed to me that there was something essentially childlike about this person. I do not find it particularly difficult to accept someone in that state.

Masson is not alone in questioning the achievability of unconditional positive regard. Even Rogers stated that to hold someone in unconditional positive regard is 'sometimes very difficult' (Rogers, quoted in Hobbs 1987: 20). Writing from within the person-centred approach, albeit towards the experiential psychotherapy end of the continuum, Lietaer (1984) examines the controversy which surrounds unconditional positive regard, stating (p. 41): 'unconditional positive regard is probably one of the most questioned concepts in client-centered therapy'. He considers that unconditionality has its problems (1984: 41). These Lietaer lists as:

(1) There is a potential conflict between genuineness or congruence on the one hand, and unconditionality on the other; (2) It is a rare person and a rare time in which the constancy of acceptance can be provided by any therapist for any client. Thus, while unconditionality is not impossible, it is improbable; (3) Unconditionality calls upon the therapist for a devoted self-effacing that often leads to a compensatory reaction in which confrontation becomes a form of self-assertion.

Lietaer sees that these questions and difficulties arose as client-centred therapy became more relationship-centred with a resulting increased prominence given to the therapist's congruence ('which implies among other things feedback and confrontation'). Bozarth (1998: 85) believes Lietaer to be in error and expresses the view that 'client-centred' and 'relationship-centred' are not differently defined and that Lietaer's 'behavioral definition of genuineness as involving feedback and confrontation' leads to a shift in emphasis from trusting the client's experience towards trusting the 'expertise' of the therapist. I am inclined to accept Bozarth's view.

In terms of theory and my own experience (see Wilkins 2000a: 33–4), I understand the communication of unconditional positive regard to be the active facilitator of constructive change (the actualising tendency of the client is the actual agent). Although others (for example Bozarth 1998: 88, who refers to unconditional positive regard as 'the core curative condition in Rogers' theory') share this view, there is little or no confirmation from research. Indeed, in a recent effort to find research studies of unconditional positive regard, I could find only the study of Kilborn (1996: 14–23). Quite why this should be I am at a loss to say, but Watson and Sheckley (2001: 185) state that it has been attributed to 'a number of factors, including the difficulty of defining the construct, poor research tools, and increased interest in the working alliance'. Whatever the reason, I do think there is a fruitful field here for exploration. Watson and Sheckley (p. 193) point out that there have been few qualitative studies of unconditional positive regard which they regard as 'essential to help investigate the participatory nature of unconditional positive regard and the transformations in self processes that are associated with this kind of acceptance because quantitative methods fail to capture non-linear relationships'. They state that qualitative research would be necessary in the exploration of (after Watson and Sheckley 2001: 193):

- the relationship between therapists' trust and belief in the actualising tendency and their ability to embody acceptance
- the spiritual nature of unconditional positive regard
- the ways that therapists can develop unconditional positive regard towards themselves and be in the present moment with their clients.

I am sure this is not an exhaustive list.

Empathy – an Illusion of Shared Consciousness?

'Empathy' is not a concept unique to person-centred theory and it has been variously defined and valued (see Wilkins 1997a: 3–5). Duan and Hill (1996: 261–3) review the literature on empathy and consider its history and various definitions, finding it to be complex. But in terms of person-centred theory, 'empathy' does have a particular meaning. In person-centred terms, empathy is 'to sense the client's private world as if it were your own, but without ever losing the "as if" quality' (Rogers 1957: 101). It is a process, not a technique. Rogers (1975: 4) defined this process thus:

> The way of being with another person which is termed empathic has several facets. It means entering the private perceptual world of the other and becoming thoroughly at home in it. It involves being sensitive, moment to moment, to the changing felt meanings which flow in this other person, to the fear, rage or tenderness or confusion or whatever that he/she is experiencing. It means temporarily living his/her life, moving about in it without making judgements, sensing meanings of which she is scarcely aware, but not trying to uncover feelings of which the person is totally unaware, since this would be too threatening. It includes communicating your sensing of his/her world as you look with fresh and unfrightened eyes at elements of which the individual is fearful.

This sounds like asking a lot and indeed Rogers goes on to write, 'being empathic is a complex, demanding, strong yet subtle and gentle way of being', but I take the view (see Wilkins, 1997a: 8–9) that the ability to be empathic is a common human trait which has evolutionary advantages. This ability can be lost or masked but it is (given effort and personal growth work) recoverable. However, it remains demanding – but it can also be richly rewarding.

The notion of empathy too has its critics. Williams and Irving (1997: 274) take the view that empathy is not:

- a personal state or a 'way of being' of the counsellor
- a catalyst or entity brought by the counsellor to the counselling relationship
- a process engaged in by the counsellor (without reference to the client's involvement).

They see their last statement above as contradicting the definition given by Mearns and Thorne (1988: 39) and stress that empathy is a product of the encounter (it takes two to tango). They write (p. 274): 'empathy is an emergent property of the relationship which has no existence separate from it'. The process of empathy they see as dependent upon the communication of empathic understanding. I do not see any conflict here with person-centred theory – I think what they say accords with the sixth condition. It seems that their intention is to clear up misconceptions rather than argue with the core tenets. I too have argued (Wilkins 1997a) that empathy is essentially a communication process, but others (for example Bozarth 1998: 61) take the view that 'Rogerian empathy is not necessarily the same as "communication" of empathy'. I think this difference is semantic rather than real. Condition 6 requires in the 1957 version that empathy be communicated to the client and in the 1959 version that it is perceived by the client. For me, anything which can be perceived is communicated – although perhaps not deliberately. I see little difference between the 1957 and 1959 statements of condition 6 but I suspect others understand 'communication' to be something more active, even directive, and therefore not in line with classic client-centred therapy.

Empathy is probably the most written about and researched of the six conditions. Rogers (1975: 5–6) published a review of empathy research, the findings of which may be summarised thus:

- The ideal therapist is first of all empathic.
- Empathy is correlated with self-exploration and process movement.
- Empathy early in the relationship predicts later success.
- The client comes to perceive more empathy in successful cases.
- Understanding is provided by the therapist, not drawn from him.
- The more experienced the therapist, the more likely he is to be empathic.
- Empathy is a special quality in a relationship, and therapists offer definitely more of it than even helpful friends.
- The better integrated the therapist is within himself the higher degree of empathy he exhibits.

- Experienced therapists often fall far short of being empathic.
- Clients are much better judges of the degree of empathy than are therapists.
- Brilliance and diagnostic perceptiveness are unrelated to empathy.
- An empathic way of being can be learned from empathic persons.

The person-centred view of empathy has been confirmed by researchers from outside the approach. Duncan and Moynihan (1994: 295), for example, from a consideration of psychotherapy outcome research find empathy to be a process, not a therapist behaviour:

> Empathy, then, is not an invariant, specific therapist behavior or attitude (e.g., reflection of feeling is inherently empathic), nor is it a means to gain a relationship so that the therapist may promote a particular orientation or personal value, nor a way of teaching clients what a relationship should be. Rather, empathy is therapist attitudes and behaviors that place the client's perceptions and experiences above theoretical content and personal values ... empathy is manifested by therapist attempts to work within the frame of reference of the client.

In their review, Duan and Hill (1996: 270) make a plea for further research:

> Various situational factors and cultural differences need to be considered in understanding the therapeutic empathic experience, and the role of such empathic experience needs to be understood through researching the conditions under which empathy is helpful. The fact that empathy research is still plagued by various theoretical and methodological insufficiencies clearly extends an invitation for creative and persistent researchers to exert their scientific effort and contributions.

Although we take a particular view of empathy, there is no reason why these 'creative and persistent researchers' should not be person-centred.

In fact, empathy continues to intrigue therapists of many kinds, and explorations and reconsiderations of it are many. Bohart and Greenberg (1997) present as an edited collection a comprehensive 'reconsideration' of empathy, establishing its historical context in the practice of psychotherapy and offering views from client-centred, experiential, psychoanalytic and 'other recent' perspectives. Within the person-centred approach, too, attempts to understand empathy and how it operates continue. Brodley (1996: 22–30) writes about empathic understanding and feelings; Warner (1996: 127–43) has shown how 'empathy cures'; Neville (1996: 439–53) uses the work of the Swiss cultural philosopher Jean Gebser as a basis for describing 'five kinds of empathy'; McMillan (1997: 205–9) has discussed how empathy occurs; Binder (1998: 216–30) writes of its significance when working with psychotic clients; and Brodley (1998a: 20–8) gives criteria for making empathic responses. More recently, Haugh and Merry (2001) have presented an edited collection of papers on empathy from across the broad spectrum of the person-centred tradition. This covers historical perspectives, ideas on the theory and practice of empathy from classic client-centred and experiential traditions, and how empathy fits in to a wider context and links with the other conditions. In short, the case for the importance of empathy in the therapeutic process is strong and evidence for it and understanding of its usefulness continue.

Congruence – an Impossible Way of Being?

Congruence is perhaps the most widely misunderstood of person-centred concepts. This seems to be because congruence does not involve the counsellor in *doing* anything. It is a way of being. Not only that but it is not something that happens in relation to a client – it is not a product of the therapeutic relationship (although 'state of being' is something which may be affected by that relationship). It is possible to be congruent alone. There is a tendency for adherents of other approaches (and, to be fair, some practitioners who consider themselves to be person-centred) to reframe congruence as a skill or therapist behaviour – after all, if it is a necessary condition, it must involve some interaction with the client, must be about saying or doing something. But action is not called for, whereas a matching of awareness and experience (external and internal) *is* required. To reiterate, congruent therapists are not necessarily *doing, saying* or *expressing* anything; they are *being* totally themselves and are fully present and aware of the flow of their experiencing.

Haugh (1998: 45) considers the function of congruence in terms of person-centred theory. She notes that, rather than allowing the client to experience the therapist 'as real and genuine, the function of congruence lies in facilitating the therapist's ability to be empathic with, and to hold unconditional positive regard toward the client'. Being congruent is not about communicating the feelings and experiences of the therapist to the client. It is not about being honest in the sense of disclosing or being direct, blunt or whatever although, sometimes one or more of these things may be necessary to maintain congruence. Mearns and Thorne (1999: 92) express concern about the tendency of some therapists to reframe congruence as a requirement to *express* thought or feeling. They write:

... we need to draw attention to the danger of the counsellor ... slipping into the phenomenon which we call 'splurging congruence'. This depicts a pattern where the counsellor is customarily incongruent with her client over long periods of time then discharges all that pent-up unexpressed feeling in one large lump of projective material. The splurging may be done in the name of 'being congruent', but the motivation is generally punitive and is certainly experienced that way.

Lambers (in Mearns and Thorne 2000: 204) also warns against understanding 'congruence' as equivalent to 'being real'. She acknowledges that because we are culturally pre-disposed to incongruence and 'many of us carry conditions of worth which stop us knowing our experience', 'it is no wonder that therapists struggle with the concept [of congruence]'. She goes on:

Congruence is often equated with the direct expression of feeling. In person-centred gatherings the person who shows feeling (particularly of sadness or pain) is often praised as being 'real' and 'congruent'. This is a simplisitic and inadequate understanding of congruence. It focuses on 'expression' more than 'experiencing'.

In this, Lambers eloquently and succinctly denies the myth that being congruent is about voicing feeling reactions, about giving open expression to the innermost workings of heart and mind. To assume that the requirement for congruence does demand open expression of feeling and to act on it is not only mistaken but maybe it does person-centred therapy no favours.

Haugh (1998: 45–6) also suggests that 'if congruence is taken to mean, in its simplest definitions, that experience is available to awareness' then it is a necessary requirement for 'many other orientations of counselling'. She specifically mentions Jungian analysis, transactional analysis and gestalt therapy as demanding this of their practitioners. Haugh may be right about this equivalence but I think this leads some others into the error of confusing congruence and countertransference because the latter also requires attending to inner processes. Wheeler and McLeod (1995: 287) see that there is a question of 'congruence vs. countertransference' and I have quite commonly heard the two equated (see Wilkins 1997b: 36). I am clear that these are different. It seems that whichever of the many definitions of countertransference is taken, it is still a *process* involving the therapist's reaction (conscious and/or unconscious) to the client, whereas definitions of congruence stress awareness and the harmony between inner and outer experience.

Although it is *being* which is important in congruence, Rogers repeatedly made reference to at least the willingness to *express* feelings and attitudes (see, for example, Rogers 1980: 116, and in Kirschenbaum and Henderson 1990a: 119, 135). This has led some (erroneously in the view of Haugh 1998: 46, and Bozarth 1998: 74–8) to work towards determining therapist behaviours which would convey the therapist's congruence. In this respect, there is disagreement among practitioners of the person-centred approach and perhaps especially between those who adopt a classic client-centred position and those who consider themselves to be experiential therapists. For example, Lietaer (1993: 18) declares that 'genuineness' has two facets, an inner one he calls 'congruence' which is about 'being' and the availability of experience to awareness, and an outer one he names 'transparency' which 'refers to the explicit communication by the therapist of his conscious perceptions, attitudes and feelings'. Lietaer explores this difference usefully and extensively, and later in the paper (pp. 38–42) makes suggestions for practice. Coming from a different theoretical perspective, Tudor and Worral (1994: 198) also tease apart congruence, identifying four components. These they call:

- self-awareness
- self-awareness in action
- communication
- appropriateness

The first two elements share much with 'congruence' as described by Lietaer, but they argue that congruent communication involves more than transparency. They state that *apparency* 'which has a more active, relational, transitive quality' is an important aspect of congruence. Being apparent is to do with the *appropriate* communication of the therapist's experience. As indicated above, Bozarth (1998) and Haugh (1998) seem resistant to this subdivision of congruence. Brodley (1998b: 83–106) adopts a similar position to them and discusses 'congruence in regard to communication' (pp. 87–91). Wyatt (2000: 52–68) considers these positions in her own exploration of congruence as 'multi-faceted'. She writes (pp. 66–7):

The facets [of congruence] include an openness to experiencing, an awareness of experiences free of denial and distortions, the therapist's behavior, and an ability to offer genuine empathic understanding and unconditional positive regard. The 'whole beyond the facets' means a healing potential can be accessed through a belief in the actualizing tendency within the therapist, the client, the therapeutic relationship and beyond; into the interconnectedness within the universe.

In this assertion Wyatt appears to be making a claim for the transpersonal nature of congruence. This whole issue of transpersonal connection is perhaps a 'cutting edge' of developing person-centred theory (although there have been references to it for many years) and it is contentious. This, and many other aspects of the theory and practice of congruence are explored in Wyatt (2001) which is a collection representing classic client-centred, experiential and process-directed therapy views of congruence.

Responding 'Congruently' – Telling it Like it is?

Generally speaking, person-centred therapist responses are confined to attempting to convey an understanding of the client's experience but it seems that, because 'congruence takes precedence' there may be times when person-centred practitioners are required to respond from their own frames of reference. However, this notion, although widely accepted, has, at least from a classic client-centred perspective, been widely misunderstood. 'Being congruent' is not a licence for the therapist to indulge an opportunity to confront, contradict, offer an opinion or act towards the client with anything other than unconditional positive regard and empathic understanding. Congruence is a state of being and does not demand action. Haugh (1998: 49) has pointed out that, theoretically, although the therapist is required to be congruent in the relationship (condition 3), the client does not need to perceive this congruence, but 'only empathic understanding and unconditional positive regard' (condition 6). So, the therapist does not have to communicate congruence, although I agree with Haugh that it is nevertheless perceived but, I think, often subliminally. As I have argued elsewhere (Wilkins 1997b: 38) – it is *incongruence* which jars and is more likely to be directly perceived. It may sometimes be helpful to respond to a client in a way which makes therapeutic use of congruence *but* such responses are properly confined to the therapist's reaction to the client's experience. It is not considered helpful for the therapist to communicate his or her own flow of experiencing arising from any other source. 'Being congruent' is *not* the same as self-disclosing, being 'honest' or offering an emotional reaction to the client or the client's material. All of these may or may not be effective in the therapeutic relationship but they are not required of the person-centred therapist and, if they distract clients from their own flows of experience, they are likely to be counter-therapeutic.

When to 'respond from congruence' is not always an easy judgement to make (and depends upon self-awareness and practice) but Mearns and Thorne (1988: 81–3) offer 'three guidelines which would generally govern the counsellor's therapeutic use of congruence'. These are:

- It is only those feelings and sensations of the therapist which are in response to the client which are appropriate for expression.
- The response must be one which is relevant to the immediate concern of the client.
- The feelings to which the therapist responds should be those which are persistent or particularly striking.

Mearns and Thorne (p. 83) summarise their ideas thus:

> When we talk about being 'congruent' we are referring to the counsellor giving expression to *responses* which she has which are *relevant* to her client and which are relatively *persistent* or *striking*. These guidelines may appear to rule out a lot of what is conscious for the counsellor, but in fact they usually include most of the important material.

Brodley (1999a: 8–10) offers 'guidance from Rogers concerning therapist-frame responses'. She states (p. 8):

> The reasons for responding from the therapist's frame ... are (a) in order that the therapist will not be deceiving the client and/or (b) to create a process, by talking out her feelings, that changes the therapist's non-acceptance or non-empathy to acceptance and empathy.

In my view, 'congruence' then takes precedence over the other conditions only because incongruence interferes with them, that is, the precedence is one of position rather than importance in that it is (sometimes) necessary for therapists to respond from their frames of reference as a way of clearing a path to an accurate understanding and acceptance of their clients.

Although 'self-disclosure' is not the same as 'being congruent' and its place in person-centred theory is not immediately apparent, person-centred therapists do sometimes share their own experience. According to Merry (1996: 279), in the interviews he analysed Rogers did this but rarely (8 per cent of his responses were of this nature). In a study reported in 1962, Barrett-Lennard (1998: 264–7) postulated that 'willingness to be known' (through sharing personal experience) would relate to the outcome of person-centred therapy but his research did not prove this hypothesis. However, there remains among at least some person-centred therapists the sense that being 'willing to be known' can be helpful. I think that it is impossible to be prescriptive about this – self-disclosure is neither required nor forbidden. No two therapists are alike, no two clients are alike and so it follows that no therapeutic relationship is like any other. Not only that, but the nature of the therapeutic relationship changes with time. For some of us, some of the time and with some clients, an element of self-disclosure is helpful. It can aid the development of trust, it can help the client see the therapist as a real and present person, but it is important to remember that some clients just do not want to know! If it is used at all, self-disclosure should be minimal (not to obscure or disguise the therapist but because it is the client's experience which is the focus of the interaction), and only be offered if and when the therapist judges it may be helpful or, perhaps, when the client makes a direct request. Although, once again, there is no prescriptive behaviour for person-centred therapists in this respect, since we do not, for example, share with the analytic world the need for the therapist to appear as a 'blank sheet', I take the view that, if I am asked by a client a direct question about myself it is best I respond succinctly but honestly. Of course, if I feel the question intrudes on my privacy, it might be my answer is something like 'I am sorry, but I do not wish to tell you that.' Whether I reveal something about myself or openly decline to reveal something, I am showing a willingness to 'be known' as a person for I am either sharing information or declaring a boundary.

7

'Non-Directivity': A Fiction and an Irresponsible Denial of Power?

The Place of 'Non-Directivity' in Person-Centred Therapy

The person-centred attachment to a 'non-directive' approach is seen by some to be a denial of the inevitable power of the therapist in the therapeutic relationship. This argument hinges on the belief that there is an inescapable power imbalance in that relationship because in it the therapist is invested with knowledge and control while the client has neither. Indeed, according to person-centred theory, it would be argued that this imbalance is a necessary condition for constructive personality change to occur because the second of Rogers' six conditions requires that the client is vulnerable or anxious – both of which could derive from a sense of a lack of control or powerlessness. So, whether therapists wish it or not, (some?) clients are likely to follow what they perceive as directions from them. According to this argument, therefore, for person-centred therapists to pretend they are non-directive is to deny reality and this leads to an avoidance of the real issue of the imbalance of power in the therapeutic relationship. There are also arguments to the effect that, as someone with skills and knowledge, a therapist is professionally obliged to employ these in a proactive way – after all, they have spent years in training, becoming acquainted with human psychology and psychopatholgy! This is something person-centred practitioners avoid and (so the argument goes) therefore deprive and disadvantage their clients. How can this be right? Indeed, can it be ethical or moral to withhold from their clients the experience and knowledge they must have? Of course, this all depends upon how 'non-directivity' is understood.

An important early declaration of the importance of the non-directive approach is found in what Kirschenbaum and Henderson (1990a: 61) describe as the work which most influenced counselling and psychotherapy in the United States – that is, Rogers' *Counseling and Psychotherapy* (1942). One chapter of this book is headed 'The directive versus the nondirective approach' (see Kirschenbaum and Henderson 1990a: 77–87) and in it Rogers sets forth the 'characteristics of directive and nondirective viewpoints'. Rogers (in Kirschenbaum and Henderson, 1990a: 86–7) states that the basic difference in purpose between these two centres around who chooses the client's goals. He writes (p. 86):

> Nondirective counselling is based on the assumption that the client has the right to select his own life goals, even though these may be at variance with the goals his counsellor might choose for him. There is also the belief that if the individual has a modicum of insight into himself and his problems, he will be likely to make this choice wisely.

I do not think that many counsellors or psychotherapists will have much problem accepting the sentiment expressed in the first sentence (indeed, it seems axiomatic to therapy as I understand it) and that they are therefore at least part way to being 'non-directive'. However, I suppose the second sentence leaves more to discussion and debate, especially as to the source of the client's insight. Does it, for example, arise from an innate actualising tendency or the well-crafted interpretations or interventions of the skilled therapist? According to Kirschenbaum and Henderson (1990a: 62), Rogers soon began to view this early work as limited. They write of Rogers:

> He came to believe that the nondirective approach overemphasized specific counsellor *techniques,* and did not give enough attention to the counsellor's *attitudes* toward the client and how the client perceived the relationship. Gradually, he came to believe that the quality of the relationship ... [was more important in] therapeutic change than the specific techniques the therapist employed.

So, quite early on, Rogers ceased to call his approach to therapy 'nondirective' but does this mean that a non-directive attitude on the part of the practitioner became less important? The answer, in the context of the two sentences quoted from Rogers above, is certainly not. Non-directivity in the sense of assiduously avoiding imposing the therapist's will upon the client and trusting that the client will progress in the most appropriate way (that is, belief in the actualising tendency) remains at the heart of the approach.

What Does it Mean to be Non-Directive?

Just what it means to be 'non-directive' in the context of the person-centred therapeutic relationship remains a focus for debate. One view is that 'non-directive therapy' was a precursor of client-centred/ person-centred therapy and that implicit in the change of name is a recognition that therapy cannot be 'non-directive'. The other view is that non-directivity remains at the core of person-centred practice. The difference here may be more apparent than real.

Although the label 'non-directive counselling', and indeed the style from which it derived, fell out of favour long ago (Barrett-Lennard, 1998: 60, indicates that 'non-directive-reflective psychotherapy' had reached its peak *circa* 1950), there is still an assumption by some outside the approach that person-centred practitioners are relatively passive, responding only to input of some kind from the client – specifically merely 'reflecting' the client's words. This is seen to arise from Rogers' view of the therapist as a 'non-expert' and his tendency to confine his responses to the frame of reference of his client. This in turn leads to an assumption that anyone can practise as a person-centred therapist. All this is based on a misconception – Rogers did require expertise (in the sense of adherence to a form of practice in which the therapeutic conditions are at the core). The issue is about power, mystique and their misuse. It is true, however, that a tenet of person-centred theory is that person-centred therapists do not have to be trained as psychologists or psychiatrists. An accurate statement about person-centred therapy is not that anyone can do it but that (almost?) anyone who has the interest and commitment can be *trained* to do it. Implicit in Rogers' early work is that counselling and psychotherapy are not the province of a medical or psychological elite but that 'the therapeutic process could be employed by helpers in many professions' (Kirschenbaum and Henderson 1990a: 62).

Although the term 'non-directive counselling' may be out of favour, the label 'person-centred' reflecting the importance of the client and therapist in relationship, Bozarth (1998: 56-7) argues that a non-directive attitude remains fundamental to the approach and Brodley (1999a: 6) explains the theoretical basis for it. In a nut-shell, this view is that although there may be (rare) occasions when it is appropriate for therapists to respond from their own frames of reference (see Brodley 1999a: 13-22, for possible reasons) a non-directive attitude (which implies responding mainly in the client's frame of reference) is developed and maintained 'because of [the] commitment to, respect for, and trust in the client as [therapists] provide the therapeutic conditions' (Brodley, 1999a: 6). Along similar lines, Bozarth (1998: 56) asserts: 'There is, in essence, no room for directivity in Rogers' conceptions of therapy and the therapist's role. Nondirectivity casts a major influence on Rogers' conceptualization of empathy.' To me, this seems to apply more to the attitude the practitioner has towards the client than a set of behaviours. It is axiomatic that clients formulate their own goals and that the therapist is a companion on the journey, not a leader. The therapist cannot have aims for the client, cannot presume to know the desirable course of growth and development for another person. It is by tracking and responding (empathically, acceptingly and congruently) to the client's subjective experience that person-centred therapy 'works' and only by that.

Mearns and Thorne (2000: 190–1) explore the notion of non-directivity and, while they agree 'the rationale for rejecting directivity is sound' (p. 191), they offer the opinion that person-centred practitioners and theorists in their attention to directivity 'have been decidedly naive over the last 60 years'. They argue that the person-centred view of non-directivity has been essentially structural and therapist-centred whereas a functional view might be more appropriate. They state (p. 191):

> The importance of directivity is not in what the counsellor *does* but in what the client *experiences*. Whether my behaviour as a therapist looks directive or non-directive to my peers is entirely irrelevant – what matters are the functions of my behaviour. The question which should be asked is not 'is the therapist behaving directively?', but 'is the client being directed?'

This way of conceptualising the 'directivity' problem answers for me questions about the employment of 'techniques' in person-centred therapy (see below) and explains why and how, when I am sure of my clients' familiarity with me and my style and that they have a largely internalised locus of evaluation (at least in the moment), I am more likely to make responses which could be interpreted as from my frame of reference. For me, this is an important part of a move to 'mutuality' – that is, it is part of my increasing emergence as a 'person' within the therapeutic relationship. In behaving this way, I am not being (experienced as) directive – merely demonstrating my trust that my clients can and will make their own decisions using what I have to say to inform this process but not dictate it.

With reference to brief case examples, Mearns and Thorne (2000: 191–3) explore how different ways of working may be appropriate for different clients. They show that apparently highly directive therapist behaviour may not result in a directed client but, conversely, highly non-directive behaviour may cause clients to act as if directed. While I agree with them that it is the client's interpretation/experience of therapist behaviour (and intent?) which matters rather than the behaviour *per se* (that is, what is said or done cannot be separated from the context of the relationship in which it occurs), to accurately gauge the client's locus of evaluation is a delicate and complex task. In this too I am in agreement with Mearns and Thorne (2000: 194) who stress that, in order to do this, there is a need for therapists to develop 'a sophisticated, highly empathic therapeutic relationship' so that different parts (or 'configurations' – see Mearns 1999) of clients can be responded to, 'taking great care with one part to offer no process direction or reframing, while with another part, the dialogue need not be so cautious because the configuration contains an established self-evaluative function'. They go on to state (p. 194): 'if the therapeutic relationship does not contain the dimension of "meeting at relational depth", it will be virtually impossible to assess the client's locus of evaluation'. This too sounds right to me – but I want to add that I wonder if for many of us, given years of experience and enough personal work, this is a synthetic rather than analytic process – that somehow we grasp a gestalt rather than cognitively tease something apart, and base our actions on 'intuition' rather than consideration? Mearns and Thorne (2000: 194–5) seem to have a similar thought. They ask whether therapists change their behaviour as clients' loci of evaluation internalise, and affirm that of course this happens. They continue:

> That changing may not even be a matter of conscious decision-making for the experienced therapist, but will be a consequence which flows from her experiencing of the client-in-relationship: a function of both the therapist's sensitivity and her relatedness to the client.

'Directivity' and Therapist Interventions

Bowen (1996: 84–94) views 'nondirectiveness' as a 'myth' and states (p. 85) of Rogers in his (1983) interaction with 'Jill':

> He uses a much broader array of techniques than simple restatement of what the client says and clarification of feelings. He uses the client's body cues to bring her to the here and now; he uses metaphors, humors her, and exaggerates and repeats her self-deprecating comments to accentuate their absurdity and promote greater accuracy in her self evaluations. Second, he allows himself to be directive. He forms hypotheses about the source of problems and very openly checks his hypothesis. Moreover, he introduces topics, he breaks silences.

She seems to be describing Rogers in terms of Warner's (1998/ 1999: 7–8) third level of 'interventiveness'. Lietaer (1998: 62–73) takes the view that non-directivity is an impossible concept and distinguishes between direction and manipulation (he agrees with Warner that different levels of interventiveness are acceptable in the overarching person-centred paradigm).

Brodley (1999b: 79–82) takes exception to the views of both Bowen Lietaer and provides a thoughtful analysis of the importance of non-directivity in the client-centred approach, pointing out that it refers to an attitude rather than to specific behaviour. She (p. 79) observes that 'attitudes are manifested in intentions that adapt to particular circumstances – thus they cannot be rigid'. This attitude is about not exerting power over the client. But perhaps it is more than this. She further states (1999b: 81):

> The nondirective attitude is psychologically profound, it is not a technique. Early in a therapist's development it may be superficial and prescriptive – 'don't do this or 'don't do that'. But with time, self-examination and therapy experience, it becomes an aspect of the therapist's character. It represents a feeling of profound respect for the constructive potential in persons and great sensitivity to their vulnerability. Therapy is an art. As an art it involves freedom within great discipline. The mature therapist functions freely, with certain values and intentions embedded in his character and with internalized disciplines.

I think that the views of Bowen and Brodley may be easily reconciled – or at least I find it easy to agree with both positions! Rogers, in his interaction with Jill, was undoubtedly more proactive than he is usually assumed to be *but* he did not intend to direct her to a particular course of action. Here, as with other person-centred behaviours, it is *intention* that matters. If a person-centred practitioner holds the attitude which Brodley values so highly, what is actually done matters less. She makes a useful distinction between influencing clients and directing them (1999b: 79):

> The universal goal of therapy is to influence clients towards growth and healing. A therapy *must* influence in order to be effective. If it does not influence the client, any therapeutic change that occurs is *entirely* due to the client not the therapy. The nondirective issue exists at a different level of discourse from the general fact that therapy involves influencing clients. It exists at the level of the therapist's *concrete intentions* towards his client and at the level of *the therapist's awareness* of how his behavior may be perceived and experienced by clients.

For me, all this is easy to reconcile with the notion of a functional perspective on directivity.

Can the Use of 'Techniques' be Person-Centred?

Although the debate about person-centred therapy and the use of techniques is largely of interest only to the person-centred community, it is relevant to consideration of the sufficiency of Rogers' conditions and the issue of directivity. There are those who take the view that the use of any technique is incompatible with person-centred therapy (see, for example, Fairhurst 1993: 25–30; Merry 1994: 1–4), and there are those who argue from other positions. Elsewhere (Wilkins 2000b: 24), I articulate these arguments. Briefly, Merry (1994: 2) argues that 'the [client-centred] therapist's job is to attend to the client's process as his or her sole activity'. Bozarth (1996: 367) concludes that techniques may be compatible with the approach but that 'theory militates against the use of techniques', and Brodley and Brody (1996: 369) state 'one can use techniques and still be client-centred – at least sort of'. Some therapists who describe themselves as person-centred make deliberate and consistent use of 'creative' or 'expressive' techniques. For example, Natalie Rogers (1985) has developed 'person-centred expressive therapy', Silverstone (1994: 18–23) discusses person-centred art therapy and I (Wilkins, 1994a: 14–18) make a case for person-centred psychodrama. Still others allow many more responses from the therapist's frame of reference. All this is a source of discussion if not dissension within the person-centred community.

For some, any suggestion or invitation which comes from the frame of reference of the therapist is directive and therefore incompatible with classic client-centred therapy. This would include any invitation to draw, paint, dance, take on a role, etc. Others take the view that, providing the client is fully aware of the nature of the suggestions and invitations likely to be made and enters willingly into the process and the emphasis of the practitioner is on the client's actualising tendency and the six conditions, then the use of techniques extends the ways in which the latter can be offered. For me, it seems that there is a way of thinking which does not acknowledge that there is a powerful direction ('Talk to me') in classic client-centred therapy which is in reality no different from the 'directions' of the person-centred creative therapist. 'Dance with me' or 'Draw with me' seem to have no greater weight than 'Talk to me'. To avoid creative and expressive forms of therapy because they can not be person-centred is not only mistaken but potentially limiting. People express themselves in many ways other than words. To deny these expressions in therapy is to restrict and confine when 'holism' is the professed goal. I suppose a classic client-centred argument could be that if these things are important to the client, then the client will introduce them. That may be so – but is it not more likely that the client will obey the implicit 'talk to me' direction? But perhaps I represent a minority view in the person-centred tradition. However, I think the arguments Mearns and Thorne (2000: 191) put forward about the importance of the client's experience of the therapist's behaviour is relevant to the issue of techniques. This seems to echo the view of Rogers of whom Warner (1998, reproduced in the ADPCA Reader 1999: 3) points out that although he limited himself to responses which were in or close to the frame of reference of his client, he was open to the use of techniques by others. She quotes Rogers as saying in a presentation in 1975: 'If a therapist has the attitudes we have come to regard as essential, probably he or she can use a variety of techniques.' This latitude she attributes to Rogers' commitment to the self-direction of all people including therapists.

The Issue of Power: The Myth of Mutuality?

Power has long been a contentious and difficult issue for person-centred therapists – but, in its various forms and in various ways, it remains important. I believe that effective person-centred therapy depends upon therapists being fully present as powerful people who, rather than denying their power in a relationship, are acutely aware of it and seek to exercise it in a constructive, influential way. They do, however, consciously seek to avoid directing and dominating the other person. Natiello (2001: 11) seems to adopt a similar position, stating: 'I believe that a therapist needs to bring a strong sense of self and of *personal power* to the facilitative relationship.' Person-centred therapists may be seen to be interested in working towards an equality of power in their relationships, this state being sometimes referred to as 'mutuality' (see Mearns and Thorne 1988: 126–9). In a mutual relationship no one person continually dominates or leads, the views of all are heard and (ideally) action and progress are by consensus. A mutual relationship is co-operative and collaborative, people (in the case of one-to-one therapy, client and therapist) are equal within it although they may function differently. 'Leadership', in as much as it exists, will rotate freely according to strengths, abilities and needs. Because personal power can be discovered or reclaimed but never bestowed, the notion of empowering another is nonsense – Rogers (1977: 289) wrote: 'it is not that this approach gives power to the person; it never takes it away'. Although personal power can only be discovered, there is an assumption in the person-centred approach that experiencing Rogers' conditions of congruence, empathic understanding and unconditional positive regard from another facilitates that discovery. Hopelessly idealistic? Maybe – although my personal experience suggests otherwise.

Mearns and Thorne (1988: 127) argue that, as the person-centred therapeutic relationship develops, so there is a developing reciprocal trust between therapist and client. This leads to the development of mutuality which is a central process in the person-centred relationship. They write (p. 128):

From the time mutuality is established, both counsellor and client experience their work as a truly shared enterprise and they can trust each other's commitment to achieve and maintain genuineness in relation to each other.

Mutuality is highly desirable in person-centred therapy and it is a particular strength of the approach that, with its emphasis on relationship, it is likely to lead to the development of trust. Such a therapeutic relationship clearly has potential advantages for the client. Although she does not describe her thinking as 'person-centred', and her perspective is that of a researcher, Marshall (1986: 196) writes of the importance to her of 'engagement with people' as part of the research process, stating:

I seek a measure of equality and wish to be non-alienating in relationships. This involves telling participants what the project is about; discussing its aims and uncertainties; at times revealing where I stand and what I find puzzling and contradictory about the issues raised; and allowing participants to shape the research direction. Whilst, as the researcher, I have a different stake in the project from others, I expect to meet other people's needs as well as my own.

This for me is a good description of the way in which a person-centred practitioner seeks to dispel mystique and work towards mutuality.

Masson (1992: 229–47) refutes the cherished person-centred view that reliance on the therapeutic conditions and the actualising tendency results in an adjustment of the inherent imbalance of power in the 'normal' psychotherapeutic relationship, and suggests instead that while the intentions of a person-centred therapist may be sincere, hypocrisy lies at the heart of the approach. His view (as represented by Thorne 1992a: 75) is that 'the therapist who professes to be relinquishing power so that his client may be empowered is, in reality, intervening in the life of another person with powerful and manipulative intent'. Actually, I see my task in relationship (including the therapeutic relationship) to be powerful, to be fully myself, and not to relinquish my power (that would be a distortion of my reality and lead to incongruence). It is only as I accept my personal power that I can expect others to accept theirs. And, yes, I suppose in this respect I do hope to be influential but not directive.

In a way, Masson's argument strikes at the heart of the therapeutic endeavour – indeed that appears to be the purpose of his book. He believes (1992: 24) that 'psychotherapy, of any kind, is wrong' and states:

> The structure of psychotherapy is such that no matter how kindly a person is, when that person becomes a therapist, he or she is engaged in acts that are bound to diminish the dignity, autonomy, and freedom of the person who comes for help.

This is a strongly held personal view. I take another. It is my experience in the client role and as a therapist that, given the person-centred conditions, the reverse of this is true. As I have experienced the genuine, empathic acceptance of another it has been in the absence of direction from them that I have felt dignified, become more self-accepting and changed to my benefit and advantage.

Thorne (1992a: 65–6) discusses Rogers' views on power in the therapeutic relationship and advances and rebuts some of the criticisms of these views. He particularly addresses the confusion between the person-centred therapist's refusal to categorise, diagnose or in any other way to rely upon their psychological knowledge, and a lack of expertise. He writes (p. 65):

> It would be utterly wrong, of course, to maintain that Rogers in reality saw the therapist as a non-expert. On the contrary, he believed that the highest level of expertise was required by anyone who was bold enough to offer psychological assistance to another human being.

Lietaer (1998: 63) expands on this notion of person-centred expertise and points out that while client and therapist may be equally valuable, they do not enter the relationship as equals. 'This decreases the mutuality in the therapeutic relationship and makes for structural inequality.' Lietaer (1998: 65) takes the view that 'nondirective' therapy as it was originally defined was prescriptive and that these prescriptions have outlived their usefulness. He writes (pp. 66–7):

> (most) client-centred therapists have lost their directivity phobia; they no longer feel uneasy about describing their work as an active influencing process in which task-oriented responses and interventions are used to stimulate or even give an impetus to the unfolding of the

client's experiential process. They have learned to take the initiative in
an active way as process experts, without slipping into manipulation
and authoritarian control.

I am nowhere near as sure as Lietaer that 'most' client-centred
therapists would be comfortable with the notion of making 'task-
oriented' interventions. Nevertheless, there is an increasing number
of therapists describing themselves as person-centred who see themselves as 'process experts' in the meaning of Lietaer and who practise in the way he indicates.

But just what do person-centred theorists mean by power? I find
support for my notions in the work of Marshall (1984: 107–8) who
argues that there are four dimensions to power and that, as an alternative to the notion that 'power is competitive, a matter of individual
ownership, motivated towards control and expressed through doing',
'power can be co-operative, based in joint ownership, directed
towards influence and expressed in individuals' quality of being'. She
defines co-operative power as originating 'in a wide atunement to
the interests of the ... community' (p. 110). The person-centred
concept of mutuality is close to 'co-operative power'. Natiello (1990:
272) states that 'the concept of collaborative power is inherent in
the theory of the person-centered approach' and describes relationships based in it as characterised by:

1. openness (all information is fully shared)
2. responsiveness (all needs and ideas are carefully heard)
3. dignity (everyone is respected and considered)
4. personal empowerment (each person affected feels free and
   responsible to participate fully)
5. alternating influence (impact on group process moves from one
   person to another as a result of self-awareness, wisdom, experience, or expressed need)
6. co-operation rather than competition

Although Natiello was writing primarily about power in groups, what
she says applies equally to dyadic relationships.

Collaborative power is at the very heart of the person-centred
approach and it is essential that person-centred therapists actively
promote an atmosphere which is conducive to its development.
'Personal power', on the other hand, is defined by Natiello (1987:
210) as 'the ability to act effectively under one's own volition rather
than under external control. It is a state wherein the individual
is aware of and can act upon his or her own feelings, needs, and

values rather than looking to others for direction'. This power, which Marshall (1984: 231) sees as conferring flexibility and choice, is also important because its discovery is an aim of the therapeutic process. In the therapeutic conditions, the person-centred approach has a powerful tool with which to promote an atmosphere of collaboration and an increasing sense of personal power (because their implementation demonstrates a deep valuing of the thoughts, feelings and very being of the other which is seen as facilitating personal growth and maturity – see Rogers in Kirschenbaum and Henderson 1990a: 182).

Implementing and maintaining power-sharing strategies requires effort and application on the part of the therapist. Natiello (1990: 276–83) discusses 'obstacles to sharing power for facilitators' and 'obstacles for collaborative power for participants'. While she is principally concerned with group roles, what she has to say is applicable to the person-centred approach in general. Obstacles to power sharing on the part of the therapist include:

1. Abdication of personal power.
2. Failure to self disclose.
3. Distrust in the actualising tendency of the client.
4. Intention – that is, if the intention of the therapist is in some way to change or redirect the client, then power-sharing will be blocked. Conversely, if the intention is to be fully present, accepting and without artifice, then a true collaborative atmosphere has every chance of being established.

For clients, potential obstacles are:

1. Expectations and values. The therapist may be looked to as a leader or an expert.
2. Scarcity and greed. There may be an assumption that power is in some way limited and those who are greedy for it may make a bid for the role the therapist appears to have abnegated.
3. Fear. The prospect of taking responsibility, discovering personal power can be scary and so be resisted.
4. Negative image of power. If power is seen as coercive and its exercise as exploitative, then taking power may be seen as reprehensible.
5. Inexperience and habit.

Natiello (1990: 283) writes:

> collaborative power requires an entirely new set of coping skills, a whole new style of interpersonal relationship that is completely at odds with our traditional way of interacting. It is frightening to give up

the security of our accustomed ways of taking care of ourselves and getting what we need. To let go of control, for those who are used to having authoritarian power, or to claim personal power, for those who have lived subordinately, challenges our deepest expectations about security. Some may decline the challenge.

Person-centred practitioners overcome these obstacles by employing the core values of the person-centred approach, initially with respect to themselves and then continuously towards themselves and towards those with whom they are in relationship.

Person-Centred Attitudes to Power: a Block to Accurate Perception?

Although, as the discussion above illustrates, power of an appropriate type, appropriately exercised has a place in the practice of person-centred therapy, there are other difficulties associated with or arising from person-centred attitudes to power. Mearns and Thorne (2000: 216–19) consider 'the problem of power'. They express the view (p. 216) that Rogers' claim that he was not interested in power but wished to be influential was to some extent self-deceptive, stating: 'it is clear that [Rogers] wished to be powerfully influential and it is difficult to distinguish this from the desire to be powerful'. They point out that the theory and practice of person-centred therapy have compounded this problem. They argue (pp. 217–18) that there is a need for person-centred therapists to overcome their ambivalence to the exercise of power. They are not calling for any change in the way person-centred therapists behave with and towards clients. They state unequivocally (p. 217):

We wish to empower and not to disempower through the imposition of our own perceptions and prejudices. For us it is the very cornerstone of our practice that we cherish and respect the uniqueness and powerfulness of our clients and seek to facilitate a process whereby they come to recognise and own their personal power and not to be the slaves of the expectations, needs and demands of others.

Rather, they see that person-centred attitudes to do with eschewing the *abuse* of power have diminished the ability of person-centred practitioners and theorists to *use* power appropriately. This has done person-centred therapy no favours 'in the hurly-burly of the therapeutic market place' (p. 217). They take the view that:

Once person-centred therapists can overcome their ambivalence about the exercise of power, they will be able to attend fully to the self configuration which tells them, with conviction, that their approach works and that it is based on an understanding of human development and human relationships of which the world stands badly in need at this juncture.

I am with Mearns and Thorne in their belief we must overcome our ambivalence to the exercise of power. It is time for the person-centred approach to emerge from the shadows in which we, its thinkers and doers, have unintentionally melted. To advance, to do our best for ourselves, our clients, potential clients and perhaps society as a whole we need to be powerfully and passionately present in a variety of professional settings. We need to speak in such a way as to be heard by those who have been deaf to our whisperings, we need to bring our skills to the activity of researching therapy in general and our approach in particular so that we may demonstrate what we 'know'. Given a willingness to own our personal power and to exercise collaborative power, as Mearns and Thorne (2000: 219) point out 'the opportunities ahead are ... abundant'.

8
An Absent Psychopathology: A Therapy for the Worried Well?

Person-Centred Therapy and 'Mental Illness'

There is an assumption that the person-centred model of the person, a commitment to a non-directive approach and a dislike of labelling means that person-centred theory can take no account of 'psychopathology'. This is seen as restricting its applicability to clients with mild neuroses and acute but 'everyday' problems (bereavement, mild anxiety and so on). For some, the person-centred approach has a usefulness with people who are so deeply disturbed or dysfunctional that they are 'unsuitable' for psychotherapy (see Kovel 1976: 116). In both instances, the assumption is that person-centred therapy is relatively trivial or light and its adherents lack the skills and knowledge to deal with deep-rooted psychological problems. In short, person-centred therapy is characterised as little more than 'tea and sympathy'. Others accept that person-centred practitioners do work effectively with people who are 'mentally ill' but see this as a recent development. A colleague well versed in both the analytic and person-centred traditions said to me recently: 'person-centred people have just discovered psychopathology and psychodynamic people the importance of the relationship'. Perhaps there is some truth in both these assertions. It certainly seems true that writing about psychopathology from a person-centred perspective is relatively new (and there are still many of us who resist the term), but person-centred work with people variously labelled 'schizophrenic', 'mentally ill', etc., has been a feature of the approach since at least the time of the 'Wisconsin project' in the 1960s (see Rogers 1967: 267–8) where the efficacy of the client-centred approach with 'schizophrenics' was investigated. Although this research is now seen as 'equivocal' (Bozarth 1998: 15), it was ground-breaking in that there were discoveries about making psychological contact with chronically 'ill', long-term institutionalised people diagnosed as psychotic. Barrett-Lennard (1998: 267–70) gives a good account of the research methods and findings of this project. It was from this work that congruence was seen to be the condition which took precedence over all the others. Mearns and Thorne (1988: 94) point out that congruence is critical when working with psychotic people (who by definition are at least to some extent divorced from external reality) where a consistent, human relationship in which 'the counsellor gives the client a clear picture of her part of that external reality' is of 'paramount importance'.

If client-centred approaches to therapy are considered by their practitioners to be appropriate to clients of many kinds, and there is actual evidence that person-centred therapists can and do work with people who may be considered to be demonstrating any of a variety of 'pathological' states, why does the view of person-centred therapy as of limited applicability persist? Partly, I guess, this is because person-centred therapists have not until recently presented them-selves as having a united front in national and international forums so what we do and how we do it has not been widely known, but perhaps it also stems from our insistence that there is no difference between counselling and psychotherapy. Also, perhaps there is some truth in the person-centred view that in this (and in many other ways) person-centred theory is subversive and disruptive of the status and power of a psychotherapeutic elite and is consequently reacted to with denial and distortion of its efficacy and wide applicability?

'Counselling' versus 'Psychotherapy'

Although in the final analysis arguments about the nature of coun-selling versus psychotherapy are sterile because they are often circu-lar and based on different definitions – that is, 'psychotherapy and counselling are the same [or different] because I believe them to be' – it may be that these arguments do have something to do with how person-centred therapy is seen as inappropriate to people thought of as mentally ill.

As I stated in Chapter 1, in terms of person-centred theory there is no difference between counselling and psychotherapy. That is, they are not distinguished by the notion of 'depth' or duration; the person-centred practitioner responds to the client and the client's subjective experience whatever it may be in the same way and with the same intent, whether they are being told of exam nerves or the most horrendous early abuse. Although there are arguments sup-porting this position (see, for example, Thorne 1992b: 244–8), there is also a widely held view that counselling and psychotherapy may overlap but actually represent stages of a continuum. This con-tinuum may even be assumed to be something like:

Advice — Guidance — Counselling — ('Therapeutic
Counselling') — Psychotherapy — Psychoanalysis

Implicit in the idea of a continuum is that there are real differences
between its separately located elements. This view is represented by
Naylor-Smith (1994: 284–6) who (with reference to psychodynamic
practice) postulates a progression from 'counselling' which may
focus on the client's life in the present, through a process in which
reference might be made to previous events of which current experience reminds the client, to a relationship in which the focus shifts
to 'the unconscious, dreams, phantasy, the transference and counter
transference, and the relationship of all this to the client's personal
history and to present problems' (p. 285). This, Naylor-Smith sees
as the area in which counselling and psychotherapy overlap. For
Naylor-Smith, psychotherapy is characterised by a shift in emphasis
brought about at least partly by meeting more frequently than once
a week. He states: 'with more frequent sessions, more focus on the
unconscious, on dreams and phantasy, and on the transference and
counter transference; and with the allowance of greater dependence
and of regression, the work is now, in my view, clearly psychotherapy'. While I am not sure that Naylor-Smith agrees with me, but I
think there is often an implicit hierarchy in this view – psychotherapy is 'better' (more powerful, requires more of the practitioner in
terms of skills and knowledge) than counselling but psychoanalysis is
best of all! To an extent, this is reinforced by the fact that, in the UK
at least, courses leading to a qualification in 'counselling' are often
of shorter duration than those leading to a qualification in 'psychotherapy'. Indeed, some training institutions offer their counselling
graduates the possibility of extending their training for perhaps
another year so that they may become psychotherapists. An approach
the practitioners of which are dubious about the transference relationship and the value of 'interpretation' and therefore the sacred
cow of analysis and who furthermore state that there is no difference
between counselling and psychotherapy runs counter to the belief
that psychotherapy (and therefore psychotherapists) has more to
offer. An easy assumption on the part of practitioners who do see a
clear distinction between these two is that, because in terms of
person-centred theory there is no difference, it can only be that
person-centred practitioners are merely doing what they would clas-
sify as counselling. From there it is but a short step to 'knowing' that
person-centred therapy is limited in its applicability, and for clients
with 'deep-rooted' issues or who are ('treatably') psychopathological
another approach is to be preferred. Perhaps a (highly compacted)

tale from my own practice will illustrate how, from a person-centred perspective, there may be a seamless flow from something which it is easy to characterise as counselling to a process more closely resembling what I think to some people is psychotherapy.

Jane, a woman in her early thirties with what she considered a rewarding career and a steady and satisfying relationship first came to me complaining of difficulty in sleeping and in concentrating. She thought that she was 'stressed' and that a little counselling might help. I thought that I could offer Jane the necessary and sufficient conditions and so we agreed to meet weekly. This was the extent of our 'contract'. There was no mention of how many times we would meet, nor of the likely course and content of our sessions.

In our first few meetings, Jane told me of events in her life and how she felt about them. I did my best to respond to Jane with empathic understanding and acceptingly, checking my perceptions by 'reflecting' – in other words, I was doing what I normally do. We had been working together for about six weeks when Jane told me that she had no memories of her early childhood. As far as she could tell, she remembered nothing from before the age of seven and her memories from then until ten years old were at best hazy and disordered. Jane said she was both puzzled and vaguely disturbed by this. It was about this time that Jane also told me she could not bear to be touched – she said this in a very matter-of-fact way. It was just another thing that made her different.

Our relationship continued and it seemed that, for Jane, some of the symptoms of stress she had been experiencing began to ameliorate. She gave no indication that she wished to discontinue our relationship and began to return more frequently to the absence of childhood memories and what this might mean. She did recall (or rather have a sense of) a relationship with someone who used to care for her in the absence of her parents. Although this memory too was annoyingly vague, nevertheless Jane had a sense of warmth and safety when her thoughts led in that direction.

Jane's story grew in detail and complexity. One day she told me that when she was making love with her partner, her experience was of being on the ceiling, watching. It wasn't that the process was unpleasant, indeed in a way she found it pleasurable – but at the same time Jane was detached from her body and her partner. This for Jane was another element in the puzzle she was trying to complete (and puzzle is a good word – to me, in many ways Jane seemed puzzled rather than actively distressed). Jane was also having many dreams which disturbed her and which seemed to hint at the childhood she could not remember. Sometimes she would tell me about these dreams, most often simply saying that she knew she had dreamt and that her dream had been disquieting but that she did not recall the detail.

And so it went on. We experienced the usual ups and downs of a therapy relationship, got stuck, had moments of exhilaration and insight, grew increasingly comfortable with each other, got irritated, wondered where we were going and so on. Off and on, Jane speculated about what might have happened to her as a child and for what reason she lacked recall but she did not reach a definite conclusion. Nevertheless things began to change and Jane seemed increasingly contented. We had been meeting for about 18 months when Jane came to the session radiantly happy. She had had a blissfully happy weekend with her partner and had been in her body as they made love. It was a delicious experience – almost unbelievable in its intensity.

We carried on meeting and my impression of Jane was that she became increasingly secure in her self. One day, as we approached our second anniversary, Jane said to me that she did not know if she would ever know what she had experienced as a child or even why she did not remember but that she had decided that this could not dictate the course of the rest of her life. Now, she did not need to know, she wanted to live her life in the present. She did not believe that she needed to continue our relationship. At the end of our last session, Jane asked if we could hug. I expressed surprise (I think this was a little clumsy!) and Jane laughed saying (more or less), 'That was then, this is now'. We did hug – it seemed the right thing to do (although, for me, it rarely is), a completion and a valediction. Some six months later, I had a postcard from Jane in which she said she was well and happy. I have not heard from her since.

I don't know if my relationship with Jane was 'psychotherapeutic' (and to be honest I don't much care) but I am sure that it was much more than a narrow definition of counselling could embrace. Neither do I know what, if anything, Jane was not remembering. I admit to sometimes being curious but I did not and do not need to know. I do not know either if this was an end for Jane. Perhaps she has returned (or will return) to therapy at some time but I am sure that somehow our relationship was at least part of the way in which she enabled herself to live more fully in the present.

Even a fairly cursory or brief look at the person-centred literature quickly undermines the view that it is not used effectively with people in need of something more intense, deeper or more long-lasting than 'counselling'. Person-centred practitioners have published accounts of their work with people who are 'contact impaired', dissociated, have a 'borderline' personality and so on. What follows are illustrations of some of the theory and practice of the person-centred approach with respect to 'difficult' clients and client groups.

Pre-therapy: a System for Establishing Psychological Contact

The first of Rogers' necessary and sufficient conditions is that client and therapist are in (psychological) contact – there is some discussion as to whether or not Rogers meant something different when in the 1959 paper his first condition required 'contact' whereas in the 1957 paper it had been 'psychological contact' which was necessary. In either case, Rogers' first condition may imply that counsellor and client must be capable of at least a limited degree of mutual communication. This implies that person-centred therapy may not be useful with people whose contact with the world is impaired or limited. This would perhaps include those who are experiencing severe learning difficulties or who are schizophrenic. But the requirement for a level of understanding by the client of the therapist may not be as high in person-centred therapy as, for example, in psychodynamic counselling where it is usual to expect that for successful therapy the client must be able to understand the interpretations of the therapist.

In fact there is a well-developed person-centred system of thought embracing clients with severe learning difficulties and schizophrenia which Prouty (1976, 1990, 1998) calls 'pre-therapy'. One of the basic ideas here is that, with some clients, 'psychological contact' may not be assumed. Pre-therapy offers a strategy for establishing psychological contact. Briefly, at an initial level this involves contact reflections which are of five forms. These are (after van Werde 1994: 122):

- *Situational Reflections* – people, places, things and events are reflected ('the sun is shining', 'you are in my office') with the intention of restoring or strengthening clients' contact with their immediate environment.
- *Facial Reflections* – the emotion implicitly shown by the client's facial expression is reflected ('you smile', 'Peter looks angry') so that the client may contact and express pre-expressive feeling.
- *Body Reflections* – what the client is physically doing is reflected, perhaps in words ('you have your hand up') or perhaps by mirroring the client's behaviour (the therapist rocks in his seat in the

same manner as the client). Such reflections assist clients to develop an immediate sense of their bodies and also helps to form some 'here-and-now' reality contact.

- *Word-for-Word Reflections* – words or other sounds which are socially comprehensible or which seem meaningful to clients are reflected back to help them experience themselves as expressors and communicators and in that sense they work towards restoring functional speech.
- *Reiterative Reflections* – any previously successful reflections are repeated in order to strengthen such contact as has been established and to further facilitate the experiencing process ('I said "floor" and you looked at me'; 'You looked at my watch and I said it was 3 p.m.').

Prouty (1998: 80) considers that the 'primary application' of pre-therapy is to '"contact impaired", regressed, low functioning and chronic clients, such as the developmentally disabled, schizophrenic, dissociated or Alzheimer's populations'. In this paper, he also discusses (sometimes with 'vignettes' drawn from practice) pre-therapy work with regressed, autistic, 'multiple personality' and voice-hearing clients. This is a comprehensive list of 'psychopathological' types. Van Werde (1994: 121–5) provides an accessible introduction to pre-therapy, describes some of the key processes and gives some succinct but helpful case illustrations.

Person-Centred Therapy and 'Severe Disturbance'

Prouty is not alone in having developed ways of working with particularly 'difficult' or 'damaged' clients. Lambers (1994: 105–20) writes on 'person-centred psychopathology'. She discusses person-centred ways of understanding and working with neuroses, borderline personality disorder, psychoses and personality disorders. Hutterer et al. (1996: 481–546) include a section on 'severe disturbances' which comprises six papers covering working in a person-centred way with people diagnosed as schizophrenic, clients who had experienced early trauma, people with learning difficulties and simply those who are 'very disturbed'. Binder (1998: 216–30) discusses the use of empathy with psychotic clients. The work of Warner too merits mention. She has developed 'process' models for clients with a variety of challenging 'problems' and behaviours – these demonstrate a person-centred way of thinking about groups of people who may (in terms of other models) be categorised as ill or disturbed. She has described (Warner 2000: 144–71) 'fragile process' and 'dissociated process'. Fragile process, she writes (p. 145),

> is a style of process in which clients have difficulty modulating the intensity of core experiences, beginning or ending emotional reactions when socially expected, or taking the points of view of other people without breaking contact with their own experience. Clients in the middle of a fragile process often feel particularly high levels of shame and self-criticism about their experience.

Warner (p.144) indicates that people who have a fragile style of process may, in terms of other models, often be diagnosed as having borderline, narcissistic, or schizoid personality disorders, and be seen as using archaic defences such as splitting and projective identification. Warner (p. 150) sees the roots of fragile process as in 'empathic failure in childhood' and that 'empathic understanding responses are often the only sorts of responses people can receive while in the middle of fragile process without feeling traumatised or disconnected from their experience' (p. 151). Dissociated process she describes (p. 145) as:

> a style of process in which aspects of the person's experience are separated into 'parts' – personified clusters of experience which may be partially or totally unaware of each other's presence. These parts have trance-like qualities, allowing the person to alter perceptions, to alter physiological states and to hold contradictory beliefs without discomfort.

Dissociated process is likely to have arisen to protect the person from blocked memories of intensive childhood sexual or physical abuse. What is important when working with clients in dissociated process is extending the therapeutic conditions (again, Warner 2000: 165, emphasises the value of empathic understanding) to *all* the parts of the client. This is essentially similar to Mearns' (1999: 125–30) ideas about working with configurations of self. Warner also refers to a third type of processing which she has observed in clients whose experience is often difficult to handle or overwhelming for psychotherapists – this she calls 'psychotic process'. As I understand it, a paper about this third process type is in production. My supervisees who work in a person-centred way with people with eating disorders find Warner's ideas and strategies concerning dissociated process particularly useful.

There are also many accounts of person-centred work with clients of types which might seem to merit particular interventions, certainly clients whose issues take them far beyond 'the worried well'. Wilders (1999: 93–100), for example, writes of the relevance of the person-centred approach to working with 'substance users', Farrell (2000: 115–21) also writes about 'addiction' and Hawkins (2000: 122–7) considers that the person-centred approach makes a special contribution to working with survivors of childhood abuse. Pörtner (2001: 18–30) discusses person-centred therapy with people with special needs. She states (p. 19):

There is obviously a need for psychotherapy for people with special needs. But how can psychotherapy cope with the specific demands of working with these clients? As much as the person-centred approach is meeting those demands, client-centred psychotherapists cannot just work in their usual way, but have to think about what might be different in terms of conditions and focus, and about how to modify their therapeutic work without giving up client-centred principles.

She goes on to explain how this can be done.

There is sufficient evidence to establish that it is not that person-centred practitioners confine their therapeutic endeavours to working with the 'worried well', but it has been true to say that, until recently, there has been little effort made to describe strategies for working with clients who in terms of the medical model (and for me this includes any approach which attempts to reach a diagnosis) may be thought of as being 'ill' or 'damaged'. Recent endeavours to describe ways of working with such clients and to establish 'theory' relevant to the development of psychopathological states probably reflects real developments but it also seems to be a response to an increasing anxiety among person-centred practitioners that they are not seen as psychotherapists by others who adopt this label. Until recently this mattered less, but the increasing influence of insurance companies in (especially) continental Europe and the USA has heightened awareness of what might be seen as a lack of credibility brought about by an ignorance of our ways. For many person-centred practitioners this came to a head at the first international congress for psychotherapy held in Vienna in 1996 where, because the approach was not represented by an international body, they felt marginalised and dismissed, while approaches with far fewer adherents and a less developed track record of theory and practice were apparently accorded higher status *because* they were so represented. This led directly to the establishment of the World Association for Person-Centered and Experiential Psychotherapy and Counselling.

9
Reflection: A Simple Technique of Little Effect?

It is not only the theory of person-centred therapy which is subject to criticism – so too are some of the practices of the approach. For some people, the absence of technique, and what is seen as a reliance on 'reflecting back', suggest that person-centred therapy is so simple that not only can anyone do it but it is unlikely to have any effect. Indeed, in the beginning stages, this is often the attitude of the students I train in the practice of counselling skills. They can see little or no point in 'parroting' the words they have heard from the person to whom they are listening when all too obviously some much more purposeful and focused intervention is required! It is only with practice and time that they begin to appreciate the extreme subtlety of reflecting content and reflecting feelings. They eventually recognise that far from parroting their clients, they are checking their own perceptions as to what is being said or experienced and communicating their willingness to understand. Even then, it takes a while for them to appreciate the effects of this on the client – even though in the client role they value the experience. Although I am not training my students to be 'person-centred', they are introduced to the principal skill of person-centred therapy which, as Merry (2000: 351) states, 'is sometimes referred to as reflection of feelings'. I agree with Merry that although this term is in some ways useful, it is also misleading because it is only a partial description of the process. Just what 'reflection' means to person-centred practitioners, how we do it and what we think happens because of it is worthy of examination and expansion.

What is 'Reflecting'?

For many therapists, reflecting is a technique – or perhaps a set of skills. This is the position taken by (for example) Culley (1991: 41–9) who sees 'reflective skills' as comprising restating, paraphrasing and summarising. She says of these skills that they are the most useful a counsellor has, and:

They provide a medium for communicating empathic understanding and acceptance in a way which probing skills do not. Using reflective skills will enable you to track clients' thinking and feeling; to check in a non-intrusive way that you have understood and to impose minimal direction from your frame of reference.

If we assume that condition 6 has the same meaning in Rogers' 1957 and 1959 statements, 'communicating empathic understanding and acceptance' is in accord with the aspirations of a person-centred practitioner, but the way Culley goes on to describe even these 'non-intrusive' skills indicates subtle (and sometimes not so subtle) divergences in intention and practice from that of the person-centred therapist. For example, she refers (p. 42) to reflection as a way of reminding the client what they were saying, gaining information and (in the form of a summary) beginning a session. All of these introduce something from the therapist's frame of reference and so depart from the non-directive stance favoured in person-centred work. So, if person-centred therapists are not using 'reflecting' in this way and for these purposes, what do they intend? If we let 'reflecting feelings' stand for reflecting in general, there are some very explicit statements about this.

Rogers (in Kirschenbaum and Henderson 1990a: 127–8) expressed his dissatisfaction with the notion of 'reflecting feelings'. He stated clearly:

I am *not* trying to 'reflect feelings.' I am trying to determine whether my understanding of the client's world is correct – whether I am seeing it as he or she is experiencing it at this moment. Each response of mine contains the unspoken question, 'Is this the way it is in you? Am I catching just the color and texture and flavour of the personal meaning you are experiencing right now? If not, I wish to bring my perception in line with yours.'

For therapist responses which would normally be labelled as 'reflecting feeling', Rogers preferred the terms 'testing understanding' or 'checking perception'. I suggest these terms are just as appropriate to 'reflecting back' of any kind – the therapist's intention must always be to ask the (implicit) questions 'Have I understood you? Is this you what you are experiencing?' I guess there is also an implicit assertion: 'even though my understanding of your experience may be accurate, my unconditional positive regard is in no way diminished'. As Merry (2000: 351) points out, the experiences to which a person-centred therapist responds are not confined to 'feelings', but 'may include, for example, thoughts, bodily sensations, fantasies and memories, etc.'

Not all person-centred practitioners are unhappy with the term 'reflecting feeling'. Shlien (in a letter to Rogers in 1986) offered what Thorne (1992a: 50) refers to as 'a spirited defence of the concept'. Rogers (in Kirschenbaum and Henderson, 1990a: 127) quotes Shlien thus:

> 'Reflection' is unfairly damned. It was rightly criticized when you described the wooden mockery it could be in the hands of insensitive people, and you wrote beautifully on that point. But you neglected the other side. It is an instrument of artistic virtuosity in the hands of a sincere, intelligent, empathic listener. It made possible the development of client-centered therapy, when the philosophy alone could not have. Undeserved denigration of the technique leads to fatuous alternatives in the name of 'congruence'.

Exactly what person-centred therapist are doing when they 'reflect' is by no means trivial, but runs to the heart of person-centred theory. Firstly, there is the matter of 'non-directivity'. That person-centred practitioners are non-directive refers to their *attitude*, not to their behaviour (see Chapter 7). It seems to me that if, when I reflect, I have the intention of holding up a mirror to my clients so that they may see themselves (presumably with the notion that something will happen as a result) then I have moved away from my prime task (which is to understand my client's experience and to communicate that understanding with empathy and acceptance), and begun to operate from my frame of reference. On some level and in some way I will have taken the decision 'you should see/hear this'. I am in effect 'doing' something to my clients rather than accompanying them on their journeys. There is a direction here, certainly a moving away from the perceptual world of my client and from the 'necessary and sufficient conditions'. If, on the other hand, when I 'reflect' my intention is to check my perception of what is being experienced and to communicate my empathic understanding and unconditional positive regard, then I am endeavouring to stay close to my client's experience. This *does* accord with the therapeutic conditions (specifically the sixth). It is axiomatic to person-centred therapy that attitude and intention matter – the implication is that, in some way, clients know the motivation behind any therapist behaviour. If clients understand 'reflecting back' as a clever trick on my part to get them to focus on some particular feeling, thought, sensation or other kind of experience, then this will have a different effect than if they understand me to be checking that I understand them. My 'reflecting' responses may be to the words the client has used (in the most concrete and direct way of reflecting I may use only words I have heard), to the feeling being expressed (which perhaps I perceive largely through 'non-verbal' communication) or in response to my empathic sensing. So, person-centred therapists may reflect the content of what the client has said, the feelings expressed by the client, both of these together or even the deeper feeling or meaning that the therapist perceives but which is unsaid and (apparently) unexpressed. This latter is what Mearns and Thorne (1988: 42) refer to as 'depth reflection'. It is important to understand that a depth reflection is not an offer of unconscious material perceived by the therapist but not the client. Rather it is an empathic response to something (a thought, a feeling, a sensation, an intuition) which is just below the threshold of awareness. That is, when such a reflection is made, there will be an instant recognition on the part of the client 'Yes, that's it!' Perhaps making a depth reflection is more of an art than a science – certainly it seems to be a process which, although it can be described, cannot be taught and should not be deliberately striven for. Brodley (1993: 17–18) points out that although the experience of receiving a depth reflection (not a term she uses) is, for the client, therapeutic and valued, 'it is not something for the therapist to *try* to achieve'. However, it is clear that although it may be contentious and require caution, working with 'the edge of awareness'. By making 'reflections', *is* part of the person-centred tradition. Rogers (1966: 160) wrote:

> it is not the case that the client-centered therapist responds only to the obvious phenomenal world of the client. If that were so, it is doubtful that any movement would ensue in therapy. Indeed there would be no therapy. Instead the client-centered therapist aims to dip from the pool of implicit meanings just at the edge of the client's awareness.

Mearns and Thorne (2000: 174–6) offer an advancement to person-centred self theory which takes account of the edge of awareness. They refer to Rogers' concept of 'subception' (see Rogers 1959: 204) which Tudor and Merry (2002: 133) define as 'a term … to signify discrimination without awareness' and propose (p. 175) 'a re-configuration of Rogers' concept of Self to include … subceived material'. They argue that to alter the person-centred model of the self so that it changes from being synonymous with 'self concept' to 'self concept plus edge of awareness' material may be an obvious step but an important one. In their view, to do this offers a theoretical basis for including 'focusing' 'as a dimension of person-centred therapy' and they state (p. 175): 'furthermore, it makes it possible for us to consider emerging "configurations" of Self'. Merry (2001: 43–8) also considers person-centred 'psychotherapy at the edge of awareness' and while he explains (p. 43) that edge of awareness material and subceived material 'cannot always be regarded as synonymous', he finds many parallels between the ideas expressed in Mearns and Thorne (2000) and those of Rogers. For Merry (p. 45):

> it is possible ... to conceptualise edge of awareness material as that material, not yet in full awareness but accompanied by tension and/or anxiety, which has the potential to be integrated into existing perceptions of the self, or to modify or even replace existing configurations of perceptions.

And:

> In person-centred psychotherapy, the location of an experience at the edge of awareness refers operationally to experiences that are subject to the defences of distortion or denial, i.e., those experiences that challenge the currently held self-concept, to such an extent that the experiences are not allowed fully into awareness, but are, nevertheless, in some measure impinging on the client's phenomenal field. In other words, they are making a difference, even though their content is not differentiated sharply enough for a person to describe them.

For Merry, this property of emergence is what distinguishes edge of awareness material from the notion of unconscious material, and in this he echoes Mearns and Thorne. Mearns and Thorne (2000: 175–6) warn that their proposition that the person-centred model of the self be altered to include edge of awareness material is radical and potentially dangerous. It is radical because it 'could detract from the essentially phenomenological nature of person-centred therapy' and the danger lies in the possibility 'that this widening of the concept of Self could lose its discipline in holding to the edge of awareness and wander into the unconscious'. They (p. 176) state that 'an important and distinguishing feature of person-centred therapy is that it does not drift into the unconscious but works within the awareness and, we are suggesting, the *emerging* awareness of the client'. They point out that although some practitioners of other approaches may regard the unconscious as the repository of rich material to be uncovered for the client through the efforts of the therapist, 'much is lost by disappearing into the unconscious'. Not least of these losses is that of the client's self-expertise and consequent disempowerment.

Although the notion of 'edge of awareness' is of great theoretical importance, as Thorne (1992a: 51) states, it is 'immaterial' what the form of therapist responses sometimes referred to as 'reflecting feelings' is called. 'Their significance lies in the fact that they typify what it meant for Rogers to translate the notion of empathy into therapeutic practice.' Primarily, then, 'reflecting' is about responding to a client empathically and, as such, an accurate reflection ensures the client of the therapist's understanding and acceptance. But reflecting has other effects too (although they are not necessarily the aim of the therapist).

The Function and Purpose of Making Reflections

On the most simple level, making a reflection is the prime way in which therapists communicate their understanding to clients. Put simply, reflecting is making a statement which encapsulates what the listener has 'heard'. To be effective, this 'hearing' must have the qualities of acceptance and true understanding and it must come from someone who is experienced as genuine in the moment (i.e. it requires the presence of conditions 3, 4 and 5). The most basic effect of being heard in this way is to facilitate further exploration, elaboration and revelation on the part of the client.

To some practitioners (of many persuasions), making a reflection is, as the metaphor implies, like holding a mirror up to the person in the role of client. And it is common for clients, even the clients of person-centred practitioners, to report their experience as if they had in some way been 'shown' themselves. Rogers (in Kirschenbaum and Henderson 1990a: 128) acknowledges this, stating:

I know that from the client's point of view we are holding up a mirror of his or her current experiencing. The feelings and personal meanings seem sharper when seen through the eyes of another, when they are reflected.

Slack (1985: 41–2) (also in Kirschenbaum and Henderson 1990a: 128) writes of her experience of being in the client role with Rogers:

It was like Dr. Rogers was a magical mirror. The process involved my sending rays towards that mirror. I looked into the mirror to get a glimpse of the reality that I am....This experience allowed me an opportunity to get a view of myself that was untainted by the perceptions of outside viewers. This inner knowledge of myself enabled me to make choices more suited to the person who lives within me.

She also tells of the importance to her that these 'rays' were not distorted by the mirror that was Carl Rogers – in other words that he confined himself to responding in her frame of reference. Anecdotal evidence (and my own experience in the client role) indicates that there is something hugely beneficial in this process. 'Seeing' one's self reflected in (or by) the therapist results in a falling away of scales from the eyes; sometimes it is as if it is only on hearing one's words on the lips of another that they are truly heard by the originator! This new vision, these new sounds can result in or contribute to constructive change. Certainly it can be a liberating experience. There are probably numerous explanations for this process (depending upon the theoretical constructs of the person offering an explanation), but in terms of person-centred theory and expressly the six conditions I think it is primarily unconditional positive regard which is at work here. Perhaps I can best explain this with reference to my subjective experience in the client role. Hearing another voice my current experience (that is, reflect my 'feeling') has, at times, resulted in profound insight. It is as if, because another is saying my words, expressing my emotion and apparently without judgement and with disinterest I can do this for myself. Somehow, my self-acceptance is being facilitated. I should emphasise that when this occurs I am not actually thinking about the unconditional positive regard the person I am talking to has for me or my positive self-regard, but rather I am immersed in some process. What I am sure about is that any hint of a lack of unconditional positive regard I *would* notice in some way, and the process would be blocked. It is likely that I am connecting in some way with the experiential source of what I have been talking about or feeling. 'Experiencing' is a central concept in person-centred therapy and was defined thus by Rogers (1980: 132):

> when a hitherto repressed feeling is fully and acceptably experienced in awareness during the therapeutic relationship, there is not only a definitely felt psychological shift, but also a concomitant psychological change, as a new state of insight is achieved.

Brodley (1996: 26) confirms this 'focusing effect' of 'reflecting feelings' (although she views it as unintentional and 'serendipitous'). She has also pointed out (p. 27) that:

> People are not aware that they are checking out their subjective flow of experience when they reflect upon their feelings, their reactions and upon what things mean to them. Such self reflection is spontaneous, not self-conscious, and is a natural process for most people.

This confirms my experience and the sense I make of it. With respect to other theoretical contributions, the process I am describing here relates also to 'the dance of psychotherapy' (see Mearns 1994: 5–13) and to the notion of 'configurations of self' (see Mearns and Thorne 2000: 101–19) in that it has been as if some part of me finally 'hears' another with acceptance and compassion. This can be understood as the result of someone else offering *both* (or perhaps more than two) aspects or 'configurations' of me unconditional positive regard and in no way valuing one more than the other.

Even though 'seeing themselves' is often the experience of clients, it is not the person-centred therapist's intention to 'show' them how they are behaving, echo what they are saying or tell them what they are feeling. Kirschenbaum (1979: 120) describes the therapist's purpose:

Reflection of feelings communicates to the client that whatever his feelings and behavior are or have been, no matter how troubling or frightening or socially disapproved of, he is still accepted as a worthy human being by the therapist.

In other words 'reflecting feelings' (in fact reflection of any kind) is one of the prime ways in which person-centred therapists achieve the sixth of the necessary and sufficient conditions; that is, that they communicate their empathic understanding and unconditional positive regard to the client.

Although, in person-centred terms, 'reflection' is primarily a vehicle for the communication of empathy and unconditional positive regard, it has other 'functions' too although these are subsidiary, the product of the process of connecting with the experiential world of the other, rather than a primary intent. Reflection resulting from accurate listening is vital to the establishment of a working relationship between person-centred therapists and their clients. By definition, if they are to be helped, clients are "vulnerable or anxious" (condition two of the necessary and sufficient conditions) and it is to be expected that this vulnerability and/or anxiety will be a feature of the relationship between client and therapist, at least in the early stages. Somehow an atmosphere of trust must be engendered, for 'constructive personality change' to occur, the client must trust the therapist and be sure that they will be attended to with understanding, acceptance and compassion. Similarly, the therapist must find a way of entering the frame of reference of the client. In simple terms, they have to get to know something of each other and their respective ways of being in the therapeutic relationship. It is 'reflecting' which provides one of the main ways in which this can be done.

When I first meet with a new client, particularly one who is unused to the counselling process or has an urgent tale to tell, I find that I automatically rely on sometimes quite simple and direct reflections to communicate that I am accompanying them on the journey on which they have embarked, and to convey my intention to attend to their story, their process, their essence. I do this in the first instance by making what may be described as 'reflections of content'. That is, I respond to the words I have actually heard, perhaps to the sense of them, perhaps by using them myself. Of course, as with any other reflecting response, my intention is to be sure I have understood but I think this is also partly because I am discovering how to connect with the perceptual world of my client (so proceeding gently and tentatively) and partly because it seems to me that my client may need to know that I have heard the tale I am being told. Usually my responses are brief, my intention being to say 'I have heard, I am with you, this is what I think you mean, am I right?' but I have discovered for myself that it is sometimes important to use the actual word the client uses, and sometimes it is important to use a different one. Firstly, I have developed 'the rule of three'. If I hear from my client the same word three or more times, especially if I think I have responded to it (but perhaps by using a different word), then it is important that I too use it and in the same way. There is something important about the word (I confess I don't always immediately understand what) and it is equally important that I convey I have heard it. Almost always the reiteration stops once I too have used the word. Secondly, sometimes I become aware that my client seems to be using words which do not convey the intensity of the experience I sense – then I am most likely to respond with a different word but one which *does*. A much-simplified example from my work with 'Bill' may help to explain:

Bill was talking to me about his wife. He and she had been arguing the previous night. 'We had a real set to last night – it went on for hours and I said some things to her I really shouldn't have', Bill started telling me.

'You had a really long row,' I responded.

'It was about half past six when it started and we were still at it at midnight', said Bill. 'I can't remember now just what we were fighting about – everything and nothing, I think. Well, it got more and more heated. I said some things I shouldn't – but so did she.'

'You regret what you said', I reflected.

'Yeah, well you know how it goes. But I shouldn't have said the things I did. But I was a bit pissed off – and we were due to go out – down the pub – it was quiz night, we always go', continued Bill. He was *speaking quietly and had a half-smile on his face but my inner sense was of barely suppressed rage. What he said also clicked with me – the flavour of 'shouldn't' was not regret but something somehow 'unacceptable'.*

'You really shouldn't have said what you did, but you were just so angry! And you still are', I said.

'Yeah, I said the things I did because I was angry – bloody angry', said Bill – and the anger began to dissipate as his eyes filled with tears.

Later in our relationship, it became apparent that the reason Bill 'shouldn't' have spoken to his wife was not because he regretted what he said (although he did) but because to speak to a woman in that way was to break the rules of manly behaviour.

I recognise that, in presenting this in the way I have, I run the risk of it being seen as the mechanistic application of 'technique', and certainly I don't mean to present my 'rule of three' as some universal guide to 'correct' practice. My intention is to demonstrate how I might 'reflect' and I think intention is important here. In using Bill's exact words I was recognising that it was significant to him that I heard them. In some way, he was not asking me to 'reflect' them but to make absolutely clear he had been heard by me. On consideration, I see that my early use of 'regret' in my response was at least tinged with something from my frame of reference. Bill needed me to hear that he had done something in some way 'bad'. Using his own words (but with added emphasis) proved to be an accurate and satisfactory response. My use of 'angry' in response to Bill's milder 'a bit pissed off' was an empathic response. In other words, *all* the practices I describe above I implemented with something far from a mechanistic application of technique. They are the ways in which I attempt to understand, get close to, and respond with warmth and understanding to my client's internal frame of reference.

'Reflecting Feelings', 'Checking Perceptions' or Conveying Empathic Understanding?

Even though Shlien (see p. 110 above) makes a valid point about the value of the term 'reflecting feelings', it seems that it has in some way become confusing or misleading. The terms preferred by Rogers ('checking perceptions' and 'testing understanding') aid an understanding of the instrumentality of the process but it is clear that major theorists/practitioners see 'reflection' primarily as a way of communicating empathy. Brodley (1993: 15–21) writes of 'the empathic understanding interview', offering guidelines for beginning practice. She (p. 16) characterises the procedure for such an inter-change thus:

> The therapist listens attentively to the client and *attempts to understand*, maintaining an acceptant attitude towards whatever the client is describing, explaining or expressing. The therapist *attempts to understand*, specifically, whatever the client is attempting to communicate, *from the client's internal frame of reference*, or perspective.

She continues (p. 17) :

> Empathic understanding is fundamentally a subjective experience on the part of the therapist. However, the only way in which the accuracy of such understanding of the client can be verified is by its coherent communication to the client. Thus, in the therapeutic interaction, it is necessary, from time to time, for the therapist to speak, to verbalize, and expressively communicate, what they have immediately understood from the client. This permits the client an opportunity to verify its accuracy or correct it.

Clearly what in this paper Brodley describes as an 'empathic understanding response' could also be labelled 'reflection of feelings' – although perhaps with less accuracy. However, as she points out elsewhere (Brodley 1996: 22), what Rogers meant by empathy is 'different and more complex than simply responding to feelings'. She states (p. 16):

> client-centered empathy refers to empathic understanding of the client's entire presented internal frame of reference which includes perceptions, ideas, meanings and the emotional-affective components connected with these things as well as the client's feelings and emotions per se.

Again, the potential confusion between an understanding of 'reflecting feelings' as a simple technique for mirroring an aspect of a client's being and something more holistic, for which the phrase (for some) seems to be shorthand, is apparent. It seems clear that the expanded meaning of the term is 'testing or verifying empathic understanding'. And this understanding is of clients' whole ways of being and their current experience (and their emerging awareness), whether that be emotional, cognitive, intuitive, spiritual, visceral, somatic or these in any combination. Responding to any or all of these with empathic understanding is a lot more complicated than the phrase 'reflecting feeling' can be assumed to imply. Drawing directly on observations of the practice of Rogers, Merry (1996: 275–8) distinguishes five sub-categories of 'empathic following'. These are:

- *Accurate Empathic Reflection (Second Person)* – that is statements of the kind 'You feel ...'
- *Accurate Empathic Reflection (First Person)* – when the therapist offers an understanding of the client's experience by saying something as if they were the client.
- *Formulating the Implied Question* – that is responding by voicing the question implicit in the client's words.
- *Tentative Inquiry* – that is responses which check understanding in an exploratory manner and/or by questioning sensitively.
- *Metaphors and Similes* – using an image to encapsulate the client's experience. Merry (p. 277) reports that Rogers usually only made these kinds of responses when his client had previously used the same metaphor or simile.

Responses Other than 'Reflecting'

Checking empathic understanding (i.e. 'reflecting') is the main form of therapist response used by person-centred therapists. In his analysis of ten of Rogers' interactions, Merry (1996: 275) reports that 89 per cent of his responses 'took the form of empathic following'. Although I am wary of implying 'as did Rogers, so must we all do', this does nicely illustrate the classic client-centred approach. Although the non-directive attitude incumbent upon person-centred practitioners can be taken to mean that therapist responses are largely in the client's frame of reference and that therefore 'checking perceptions', and conveying empathic understanding are the principal ways in which this is done, other kinds of responses are admissible and, at times, preferable. Firstly, questions (which by definition are from the therapist's frame of reference) are not necessarily anathema. Sometimes the motivation for asking a question is to seek clarification. This may be necessary when, for example, the therapist is confused (Was it x or y?) or has misheard or forgotten (Did you say this or that?). Because there is a clear intention to understand, to track the client's experience, these questions are minimally intrusive. Brodley (1993: 19) refers to them as 'a form of empathic following'. Interpretative or probing questions do not conform to client-centred practice and theory. When person-centred practitioners do not understand what is being said or in any other way expressed for whatever reason, it is permissible, even desirable, to simply own this lack of understanding and ask that the client repeats what was said or restates it differently. Clearly, these responses are also about tracking the client's experience and, although this is the main focus of person-centred therapy, there are times when this process is best facilitated by (initially) responding from the therapist's frame of reference – see, for example, arguments about the 'precedence of congruence' on pp. 99–100.

10
The Issue of Boundaries: Harmfully Sloppy Ethics?

Person-centred therapists (and therefore person-centred therapy) have attracted criticism because of an apparent professional and ethical laxness, and it is true that well-known person-centred practitioners have reported practices which go beyond the 'normal' bounds of the therapeutic hour in a designated place of practice. As I have explained in on p. 5, the former may very well arise from a 'mislabelling' of people as person-centred and/or that there are more person-centred therapists than any other kind; the latter is probably more to do with genuine theoretical differences. It is also possible (indeed likely) that, by accident or design, some person-centred practitioners have transgressed ethical and professional boundaries in a way unacceptable not only to the profession of counselling and psychotherapy as a whole, but also by the standards of the approach itself (these are not necessarily always the same). All orientations have their black sheep, and any of us can make a mistake. It is not these clear and obvious transgressions which this chapter addresses, but rather I explore here just what 'boundaries' mean in person-centred practice and consider Dryden's (1993: 22) assertion:

> Several leading person centred figures have demonstrated unacceptable breaches of boundaries with clients and trainees. It seems that any therapeutic approach that places emphasis on 'loving' relationships with clients and trainees alike needs to place even more emphasis on the maintenance of therapeutic and training frames. Maybe there has been too much experimentation with extending the boundaries of care.

At the heart of Dryden's complaint is not that some individual practitioners have erred but that such error is inherent in the way person-centred therapy is practised (although he does acknowledge that similar forms of abuse happen in other therapeutic approaches). This is a serious charge. I do not know who these 'several leading figures' might be and I dare say Dryden had his (good) reasons for not naming them. If the inference I draw is correct, who they are is immaterial – what is being criticised is person-centred therapy as a whole. It seems necessary to examine what are the boundaries to safe, effective person-centred practice and how, if at all, these are different from those of any other practitioner. At this early stage, I also want to emphasise that, in terms of how they operate the 'boundaries' of the therapeutic relationship, many, perhaps most person-centred therapists practise in ways which are indistinguishable from those of practitioners of other orientations. *En masse*, we are likely to agree with Johns (1997: 57) when she points out that '[c]lients are likely to be most vulnerable to unaware practitioners who use inappropriately power, seduction, influence, pressure or emotion; who are unable to identify their own needs; or who are unskilled or incompetent on any number of key dimensions', and to see these characteristics as paving the way to unethical practice. Of course, if the 'person-centred' therapist has been appropriately and adequately trained and if the total focus of therapists is truly on the client's world (as person-centred practice requires) and there is an emphasis on continuing professional and personal development, then most of these things are less likely to happen. However, it is true that, from a theoretical perspective at least, the stance of person-centred therapy is, in respect of the nature of 'boundaries', different from some others. This is because the nature of the therapeutic relationship is differently defined from the way practitioners of other orientations see it. Bozarth (1998: 185) puts it thus:

> [In person-centred therapy] the difference between client and therapist is not therapist expertise but the therapist's congruence (versus client incongruence) in the relationship and the therapist's dedication and intent of experiencing the client in certain ways; i.e., unconditionally and 'as if' the therapist were the client. The abiding person-centered ethic is to operate from these attitudinal qualities....When the therapist is this way, the therapist can be trusted to act in accord with the positive growth directions of the client.

This has implications for practice.

What are 'Boundaries' ... and Who are They for?

The word 'boundaries' is used in counselling and psychotherapy to cover a multitude of factors limiting (in the sense of providing a framework for) work with clients. Boundaries may, for example, be spatial (using a particular room, sitting in a particular chair), temporal (duration and frequency of interactions), or to do with the nature of the relationship (for example, no social interaction and most definitely no sex). There are also 'boundaries' to do with overlapping with other professionals, for example in attitudes to the involvement of medical or social service professionals and also overlapping with other therapists. 'Contracting' too has to do with the understanding and operation of boundaries. 'Confidentiality' is subsumed into the notion of boundaries as is the privacy of the therapist – although quite what the former means appears to differ according to the setting in which particular therapists work and their *modus operandi*.

As well as determining the outer limits of the therapeutic relationship, there are also 'boundaries' which operate within therapy sessions. These include those to do with self-disclosure, touch, who decides when a session (or the relationship as a whole) is at an end, and so on. Just what is the function of these boundaries and in whose advantage they operate seems to be a largely unexplored area. As a profession, we think we know what constitutes appropriate boundaries and that they operate in the interests of our clients – but how do we know this? What is the theoretical basis for, for example, 'the therapeutic hour'? For whom is it a practical benefit? I suspect (but like others, do not *know*) that the reason we most frequently meet with our clients for an hour weekly is that this accords with some sort of natural rhythm. Certainly, I find it easy to remember weekly appointments. I do not do so badly with remembering fortnightly ones, but three-weekly appointments throw me. Monthly I can remember but I experience a lack of continuity. I suppose therefore that, because they are easier to remember, weekly appointments are to the advantage of both client and therapist, and I have an intuitive knowledge and anecdotal evidence (from colleagues and supervisees) that in monthly meetings the process is likely to be something other than 'therapy' as I understand it. But I do not know that meeting weekly is the most effective way of working towards 'constructive personality change'. And why hour-long appointments? Why not 90 minutes? Forty-five minutes? And why do we work in a way which seems predicated on the assumption that all clients have the same needs in terms of boundaries (and not necessarily only in terms of time and space)? Certainly, I know of colleagues in the counselling and psychotherapy profession as a whole who now practise 'defensively', that is, their main preoccupation is to avoid falling foul of the codes of ethics of the professional organisations to which they belong. For them, the client is no longer central to the process, but a set of 'rules' is, boundaries have become structural (see p. 127) and the structure takes precedence over the person. Although I understand why, this causes me some concern. I do not wish to imply that any practitioner should be careless of ethics but it does seem that, perhaps for person-centred therapists in particular for whom the client is the prime arbiter and for whom taking responsibility for the client is anathema, there is a tension here. It seems that some ways in which 'boundaries' are operated are a matter of habit rather than demonstrable effectiveness and that they are therefore questionable. But how did they arise in the first place? There is nothing in person-centred theory which delimits 'therapy' in terms of where, how often or even under what conditions it takes place. Arguably, flexibility in these matters accords more closely with the requirements of theory although there are often practical constraints and the therapist too has rights and preferences.

Many of the accepted boundaries in counselling and psychotherapy adopted as 'received wisdom' by individual practitioners and professional organisations have been taken wholesale from psychoanalytic/psychodynamic practice. Sometimes these boundaries are related to the theoretical constructs of psychoanalysis. Bozarth (1998: 185) states:

> Most ethical assumptions in therapy are embedded in psychoanalytic theory. These assumptions are: (1) that therapists must be controlled in their behavior with clients; that is, they can not be trusted; (2) that the client is helpless in the relationship with the therapist (and that feelings are transference towards the therapist); (3) that the therapist is more powerful than the client and can easily coerce the client.

If practice is based on the idea of transference then there are implications for the nature of the relationship between therapist and client perhaps persisting long after the therapeutic relationship is over. Casement (1985) writing from a psychoanalytic perspective makes many references to the importance of boundaries – what happens if boundaries are broken and so on – but nearly always these allude to the processes of transference and countertransference. If therapists work in a way which disregards transference, or they disbelieve the notion, and/or they value client autonomy, then, theoretically at least, this implies a different attitude to boundaries concerning the nature of the client/therapist relationship. Sometimes the reason for a particular boundary is harder to discern. As I indicated above, it puzzles me why, as a profession, we seem to have fallen into a pattern of meeting with our clients once a week and for about an hour. How do we *know* this is most effective? I do not say that it is not – merely that it seems largely untested.

Jacobs (1988: 62–76) writes about the importance of boundaries in psychodynamic counselling and offers theoretical explanations for them. For example (pp. 65–7) he explains the advantages of establishing clear contracts with clients. These are to do with relieving clients of the anxiety that counselling may end precipitately, but also to ensure that the client does not break off suddenly from therapy but works through an appropriate ending. For Jacobs, contracts are also about the practical limitations on the counsellor's time. Because other clients have to be accommodated, flexibility is often not an option. With the notion that making a contract allows both therapist and client to know where they stand, from a person-centred perspective there is not a theoretical objection and the advantages are easily appreciated. It is seen as important that the therapist is very clear about the nature of the relationship on offer and the limitations to it, because this establishes 'trustworthiness'. However, Jacobs (pp. 66–7) states:

> it is the setting of boundaries on the duration of counselling as a whole, as well as on the time available in any one session, that enables the psychodynamic counsellor to work with the feelings that accompany loss and limitation.

He goes on to declare (p. 69): 'the psychodynamic counsellor regards setting limits as valuable in itself'. The use of a boundary of any kind to induce particular feelings or experiences in a client runs counter to person-centred theory and, therefore, person-centred practice is not constrained in the same way. Mearns and Thorne (2000: 31), observe that 'the person-centred approach does not take the same line on *boundaries* as do most psychodynamic approaches...In person-centred therapy we expect a more fluid, less structurally 'boundaried' relationship between therapist and client' – while pointing out the usefulness of questioning this fluidity.

The Hazard of 'Professionalisation'

There is a small but growing concern among person-centred practitioners in the UK (and elsewhere) that, because of the emphasis their codes of ethics and practice place on therapists taking responsibility *for* clients during and even *after* the therapy, and because many of the principles therein are embedded in psychoanalytic theory, for person-centred practitioners membership of the larger, general counselling and psychotherapy associations is incompatible with good practice. This works from two directions.

Person-centred therapy is concerned with (and *only* with) the 'here-and-now' relationship between client and therapist, and, as

Mearns and Thorne (2000: 31) point out, 'if there is clarity on the relationship and the work being undertaken between the therapist and the client at this moment then the person-centred therapist feels she has attended to all the relevant variables'. In terms of many codes of practice, this may leave person-centred practitioners vulnerable to a re-interpretation of events after the therapeutic relationship has ended and actions or inactions may be construed (from another theoretical perspective) in such a way as to cast doubt upon the professionalism or ethics of the practitioner being re-evaluated. *Because* of the value placed on client autonomy and the emphasis on a non-directive attitude, the position of a person-centred practitioner with respect to the ending of therapy (and throughout the relationship) may be very different from that of a therapist influenced by (for example) psychodynamic principles. If this behaviour is then interpreted in the light of these same principles, person-centred practitioners, behaving properly in terms of the theory and practice they espouse, are cast as unethical. There is a real risk that this will become an established norm – indeed, perhaps it already is. Mearns and Thorne (2000: 48) warn of this, stating: 'if the profession is to become institutionalised under present mainstream psychodynamic influence, their need for a narrowly and structurally boundaried context may require the person-centred approach to be defined as "unethical"'.

While members of the counselling and psychotherapy profession whose practice is informed by other theories may see some person-centred ways of working as 'unethical', it is equally important to realise that this works the other way round too. From a person-centred perspective, any intervention which deprives the client of autonomy, or works in any way other than to let the client discover personal power, through the development of collaborative power, can be understood as unethical. This renders the ethics of any therapist who makes an interpretation, gives a direction or acts in any other way as an 'expert' at least dubious. As Jerold Bozarth has stated (personal communication, 2001):

> The limits [of person-centred practice] are defined by the individual relationship and the dedication to the client's world. The central concept of what is unethical is the imposition of ourselves and our beliefs on the client. This makes all other therapies unethical.

Clearly, if person-centred practitioners were to cling to this interpretation of ethical behaviour, the professional associations would either grind to a halt or we would be expelled *en masse*. Yet 'ethical' principles derived from another theory *are* allowed to hold sway. There is something wrong here and it merits consideration.

It seems to me that there are ethical principles which are derived from commonly held belief or the concept of natural justice. These include the idea that abuse of power is wrong, that the service contracted for should be delivered, and so on. There are also 'ethical principles' which are derived from particular models of the person and what these imply for the practice of therapy. It makes sense to include the first in a set of principles for a diverse profession such as ours, but not the latter, for if the set deriving from one theory is adopted, adherents of another theory become defined as unethical if they practise what they preach. Thus, I do not advocate that the professional organisations construct their codes of ethics on the basis of person-centred theory, but I do question the assumption that those derived from another (unproven) theory are somehow universally applicable. In an association seeking to include therapists of many orientations, to privilege the theoretical assumptions of one orientation is a dangerous nonsense. As I wrote some time ago (Wilkins, 1994b: 207):

> We [the then British Association for Counselling] can't offer as a legitimate explanation for one of our ethical principles a phenomenon in which only some of us wholeheartedly believe and even those who do believe in it disagree as to its duration. Transference cannot be a basis for any BAC principle.

And transference is but an example.

At the moment, person-centred practitioners not wishing to operate 'independently' have a choice to make – to compromise their practice so that they can under all circumstances remain members in good standing of the general associations, take the risk of remaining members but practising ethically by person-centred standards, or to leave (or not join in the first place) any organisation in which the inflexibility of the code of practice may compel them to 'unethical' practice and instead join only one (or more) of the person-centred organisations and practice in a way which accords with their codes of ethics.

'Power' and the Boundaries of the Therapeutic Relationship

Most approaches to therapy operate from a power base of the expertise of the therapist. That is, the therapist has knowledge and technique (and perhaps even 'wisdom') acquired through years of training and supervised practice. This experience allows the therapist to 'know' things about clients and is used for the benefit of the client. These therapists are required to operate at least in part from their own frames of reference. Person-centred therapists see power as based in the client and operate accordingly, centring their practice on the client's frame of reference. Because there is a belief that clients are the best experts on their own lives and (by definition) are capable of becoming 'fully functioning', it follows that the therapist cannot be responsible *for* the client. To take such responsibility would be, in person-centred terms, to impose the will of the therapist and to deny to client the right to exercise (or fail to exercise) personal power. However well-intentioned this might be, it is counter-therapeutic and, arguably at least, unethical. This has implications for (for example) who ends the therapy, how it ends and what are the responsibilities of therapists once they no longer meet with their clients.

Because client autonomy is prized and client-centred expertise lies in the ability to be non-directive while responding in accord with the therapist conditions, it is the client who directs the course, nature and content of the therapeutic relationship. Because therapists are also autonomous people with their own personal power (which they are obligated to employ as full and present beings), some other elements of the relationship are negotiated or 'contracted' (for example, time and place of meeting) and the exercise of collaborative power is desirable and mutuality an aim. Placing the client at the centre of the relationship (as opposed to theory or technique) does not mean that person-centred therapists are somehow self-abnegating, nor that they are charged with meeting all demands clients may make of them. For example, it is possible for person-centred therapists to respond to clients from their own frames of reference. Indeed, at times the maintenance of congruence, empathy and/or unconditional positive regard may demand this. Also, in those elements of the relationship which are negotiable or contracted, person-centred therapists have at least an equal say. It may be that the 'one-hour, once-a-week' therapy session is not negotiable. Imposing this from the therapist frame is fine, providing this is explicit. It is ethically appropriate for person-centred therapists to be clear (with themselves and their clients) what limitations they bring to the therapeutic endeavour.

Because there can be no preconceptions of what clients should be or become, in terms of person-centred theory, nothing about the relationship outside therapy can be prescribed or proscribed. But does 'therapy' take place only in the agreed encounter of whatever frequency and duration? Instinctively and intuitively my response is that it does not, that therapy is a process *facilitated* by the therapist but possibly taking place largely outside the face-to-face meeting. This *does* have implications for how person-centred therapists behave with respect to their clients. Briefly, anything which destroys or militates against 'trust' is likely to be unethical. This includes any behaviour likely to be viewed as immoral, and certainly any behaviour which involves the subjugation (however subtly) of one individual to another. For me, this precludes intimate relationships of any kind with clients (perhaps as much because I would suffer role confusion as would the client), but not common social courtesies. Unless we were both clear it was part of our therapeutic endeavour, I am most unlikely to (for example) meet a client for a drink, but if we encountered each other in a social situation I would behave as I would to any other acquaintance except that I would take my cue from the client and always act in such a way as to preserve confidentiality. In such a situation, to either 'deny' my client or to presume upon the intimacy of our relationship would be to exert my power and to impose myself. This is clearly counter to person-centred principles. However, once therapy is over, things may be different.

In person-centred terms, the nature of the relationship between client and counsellor once embarked upon is not 'once and for all'. Because therapy is predicated on the assumption that constructive personality change *will* occur and that the actualising tendency will impel the client towards a state of being in which they are fully functioning, the possibility is that therapist and ex-client will be able to meet as equals and, therefore, that they will be free to encounter each other differently – whatever this may mean in the given time and place. That is to say, relationship between ex-client and therapist is mutable and, in terms of theory, nothing is predicted for it, nothing is demanded of it. Again, this puts person-centred practitioners in a very different position from those informed by psychodynamic principles. For at least some of the latter the assumed helplessness of the client with respect to the therapist persists long after the therapeutic relationship is over – and perhaps for all time. This means they can never be equals, and so 'friendship' is not really a possibility and a sexual relationship, even years later, would be seen as abusive on the part of the therapist. In terms of person-centred theory, if it was true that ex-clients were forever unable to escape the yoke supposedly imposed in the therapeutic relationship, then therapy becomes an unethical act because the client is deprived of autonomy, the ability and right to make personal choices, in perpetuity.

Because we understand 'power' in the therapeutic relationship differently, it does not follow that as person-centred therapists we assume or act as if we have licence to indulge in any sort of relationship with clients and ex-clients which takes our fancy. We and they are protected if we offer the necessary attitudinal conditions and only these. So, while I do have former clients who have gone on to become colleagues and even close friends, this is the exception rather than the rule and has resulted from very clear, mutual understanding of the transformed nature of our relationship. In other words, we have not allowed ourselves to be hamstrung by the structures surrounding practice but have used them responsibly and responsively, adopting the notion that boundaries should be fluid and fitted to the true needs of individuals rather than treated as immutable and to be enforced to the cost of individual development.

The Fluidity of Person-Centred Boundaries

What is meant by the 'fluidity' of boundaries in person-centred therapy? First and foremost what this implies is that the client and the client's individual needs are central to the therapeutic relationship. Because each client is unique, there must be the flexibility for therapists to respond in unique ways. The duration and frequency of sessions may change (because needs change) and may be different for different clients (because it is absurd to assume that Fred will always and only benefit from the same pattern as Bill), and the site of the encounter does not need to be fixed. For example, for any number of reasons it may be appropriate to meet with a client in a setting other than the normal place of practice of the therapist. Mearns and Thorne (1988: 141) give the example of accompanying 'Joan' to the graveside of her mother and do not doubt this was an important part of her process. But 'fluidity' demands more than making the occasional adjustment to boundaries of time and place. It means responding individually to individuals. In Mearns and Thorne (1988: 89), Dave Mearns describes his work with Bob, 'a war veteran whose psychological damage had rendered him mute'. There are many things in this account which (in terms of some orientations) suggest the transgression of boundaries. For example, the meeting takes place on Bob's territory, not that of Mearns, there is physical contact (initiated by Mearns) and a display of emotion in that Dave Mearns cried with 'a deep, deep sobbing'. Now, I can imagine some practitioners reacting with horror to such a story and yet I have no doubt it is a tale of excellent practice. I understand Mearns to have responded to Bob empathically and with unconditional acceptance while congruent. He did what was required of a person-centred therapist, employing the attitudinal qualities in such a way as to allow 'Bob' to meet 'Dave', and this was transforming. Mearns can be understood as having adopted a functional approach to the operation of boundaries rather than a structural approach. Mearns and Thorne (2000: 48) explain this difference and the importance of defining boundaries functionally:

The danger for person-centred therapists is that 'boundaries' come to be defined 'structurally' rather than 'functionally'. A functional analysis would require the therapist to consider, delineate and justify her actions and in that way to be accountable. On the other hand, a structural analysis would simply demand behaviours such as: not meeting the client outside the therapy room; not offering any support other than therapy to the client; not permitting the client power in determining the therapy contract; not modifying the terms of the therapy contract and not engaging with any other persons close to the life of the client.

What is important about this statement is not only the assertion that good person-centred practice demands 'flexibility' with respect to working with clients but that the actions of therapists responding as unique individuals *to* unique individuals are firstly thought through, then clearly delimited and in such a way as these can be justified. There is not a blind reliance on 'one size fits all' rules, but a requirement to deliberate upon what is best in any given situation. And this deliberation takes into account past, present and future. For example, it may be important to think through how deviating from standard means of practice may affect other things and it is certainly important to consider if (for example) agreeing to telephone contact outside the therapeutic session is a sustainable offer or in some way limited. Jenny Biancardi (personal communication, 2001) agrees with the importance of responding to clients flexibly but says when her supervisees raise this possibility, she asks them to think about their willingness to maintain any 'special arrangement' they may make. Placing the particular individual before the unspecified client in general actually requires a much higher awareness of the nature of ethical practice and the importance of behaving ethically than does reliance on a code. Almost perversely, not only is this likely to be overlooked but valuing the individual in this way can be defined as unethical. Mearns and Thorne (2000: 50–3) deal with this at some length, raising the criticism of person-centred therapy as leading to 'over-involvement' and encouraging 'client dependency'. Needless to say, they accept neither of these charges and refute them with reference to person-centred theory. They write (p. 50):

It is fascinating that ethical challenges are made on the basis of over-involvement, yet there are no codes which describe a pattern of systematic therapist *under-involvement*. It seems strange indeed that a profession which emphasises the power of relationship should not be prepared to challenge members who offer clients such a degree of detachment in the face of pain that the client experiences this as abusive.

And (p. 52):

... psychodynamic thinking in this area of 'dependency' is so perverse due to its sensitivity in regard to the ever present danger of 'transference abuse' ..., that virtually any act of human kindness would be deplored as potentially encouraging dependency. The reality is that pathological dependency is fostered by transference relationships and challenged by 'real' relationships.

Of course, 'real' relationships are crucial to person-centred therapy!

In summary: flexible, functional boundaries are essential to good person-centred practice. These can be and are operated responsibly and ethically. Usually, when they are challenged by practitioners of other orientations, this challenge is rooted in a particular theory. A theory is just that, a proposition in want of proof, not established fact. To enshrine such theories in codes of practice does not make for good ethics – the BACP 'Ethical Framework' now seems to take account of this and arguably offers more of a 'functional' approach to ethical practice.

References

Barrett-Lennard, G.T. (1998) *Carl Rogers' Helping System: Journey and Substance.* London: Sage.

Biermann-Ratjen, E.-M. (1996) 'On the way to a client-centred psychopathology', in R. Hutterer, G. Pawlowsky, P.F. Schmid and R. Stipsits (eds), *Client-Centered and Experiential Psychotherapy: a Paradigm in Motion.* Frankfurt-am-Main: Peter Lang.

Biermann-Ratjen, E.-M. (1998) 'On the development at the person in relationships', in B. Thorne and E. Lambers (eds), *Person-Centred Therapy: A European Perspective.* London: Sage.

Bimrose, J. (2000) 'Theoretical perspectives on social context', in C. Feltham and I. Horton (eds), *Handbook of Counselling and Psychotherapy.* London: Sage.

Binder, U. (1998) 'Empathy and empathy development with psychotic clients', in B. Thorne and E. Lambers (eds), *Person-Centred Therapy: a European Perspective.* London: Sage.

Bohart, A.C. and Greenberg, L.S. (eds) (1997) *Empathy Reconsidered: New Directions in Psychotherapy.* Washington, DC: American Psychological Association.

Bowen, M., V.-B. (1996) 'The myth of nondirectiveness: the case of Jill', in B.A. Farber, D.C. Brink and P.M. Raskin (eds), *The Psychotherapy of Carl Rogers: Cases and Commentaries.* New York: Guilford Press.

Bozarth, J.D. (1985) 'Quantum theory and the person-centred approach', *Journal of Counseling and Development* 64 (3): 179–82.

Bozarth, J.D. (1990) 'The essence of client-centered therapy', in G. Lietaer, J. Rombauts and R. van Balen (eds), *Client-Centered and Experiential Psychotherapy in the Nineties.* Leuven: Leuven University Press.

Bozarth, J.D. (1993) 'Not necessarily necessary but always sufficient', in D. Brazier (ed.), *Beyond Carl Rogers.* London: Constable.

Bozarth, J.D. (1996) 'Client-centered therapy and techniques', in R. Hutterer, G. Pawlowsky, P.F. Schmid and R. Stipsits (eds), *Client-Centered and Experiential Psychotherapy: a Paradigm in Motion.* Frankfurt-am-Main: Peter Lang.

Bozarth, J.D. (1998) *Person-Centered Therapy: A Revolutionary Paradigm.* Ross-on-Wye: PCCS Books.

Brazier, D. (1993) 'The necessary condition is love', in D. Brazier (ed.), *Beyond Carl Rogers.* London: Constable.

Brodley, B.T. (1987) 'A client-centered psychotherapy practice', http://uhs.bsd.uchicago.edu/%7Ematt/cct.practice.html.

Brodley, B.T. (1990) 'Client-centered and experiential: two different therapies', in G. Lietaer, J. Rombauts and R. van Balen (eds), *Client-Centered and Experiential Psychotherapy in the Nineties.* Leuven: Leuven University Press.

Brodley, B.T. (1993) 'The therapeutic clinical interview – guidelines for practice'. *Person-Centred Practice',* 1 (2): 15–21.

Brodley, B.T. (1996) 'Empathic understanding and feelings in client-centered therapy', *The Person-Centered Journal* 3 (1): 22–30.

134 References

Brodley, B.T. (1997) 'Concerning "transference", "countertransference" and other psychoanalytically-developed concepts from a client/person-centered perspective. http://users.powernet.co.uk/pctmk/papers/psyanaly.html.

Brodley, B.T. (1998a) 'Criteria for making empathic responses in client-centered therapy', *The Person-Centered Journal* 5 (1): 20–8.

Brodley, B.T. (1998b) 'Congruence and its relation to communication in client-centered therapy', *The Person-Centered Journal* 5 (2): 83–106.

Brodley, B.T. (1999a) 'Reasons for responses expressing the therapist's frame of reference in client-centred therapy', *The Person-Centered Journal* 6 (1): 4–27.

Brodley, B.T. (1999b) 'About the nondirective attitude', *Person-Centred Practice* 7 (2): 79–82.

Brodley, B.T. and Brody, A. (1996) 'Can one use techniques and still be client-centered?' in R. Hutterer, G. Pawlowsky, P.F. Schmid and R. Stipsits (eds), *Client-Centered and Experiential Psychotherapy: a Paradigm in Motion*. Frankfurt-am-Main: Peter Lang.

Cain, D.J. (1993) 'The uncertain future of client-centered counseling', *Journal of Humanistic Education and Development* 31: 133–9.

Cameron, R. (1997) 'The personal is political: re-reading Rogers', *Person-Centred Practice* 5 (2): 16–20.

Cameron, R. (1999) 'Subtle energy exchanges in the counselling relationship', in I. Fairhurst (ed.), *Women Writing in the Person-Centred Approach*. Ross-on-Wye: PCCS Books.

Casement, P. (1985) *On Learning from the Patient*. London: Routledge.

Cohen, J. (1994) 'Empathy toward client perception of therapist's intent: evaluating one's person-centeredness'. http://uhs.bsd.uchicago.edu%7Ematt/cct.evaluating. html.

Coulson, A. (1995) 'The person-centred approach and the re-instatement of the unconscious', *Person-Centred Practice* 3 (2): 7–16.

Culley, S. (1991) *Integrative Counselling Skills in Action*. London: Sage.

d'Ardenne, P. and Mahtani, A. (1989) *Transcultural Counselling in Action*. London: Sage.

Davies, D. (2000) 'Sexual orientation', in C. Feltham and I. Horton (eds), *Handbook of Counselling and Psychotherapy*. London: Sage.

Deurzen-Smith, E. van (1988) *Existential Counselling in Practice*. London: Sage.

Douglass, B. and Moustakas, C. (1985) 'Heuristic inquiry: the internal search to know', *Journal of Humanistic Psychology* 25 (3): 39–55.

Dryden, W. (1990) *Rational-Emotive Counselling in Action*. London: Sage.

Dryden, W. (1993) 'Person-centred therapy – a view from the outside', *Person-Centred Practice* 1 (2): 21–2.

Duan, C. and Hill, C.E. (1996) 'The current state of empathy research', *Journal of Counseling Psychology* 43 (3): 261–74.

Duncan, B.L. and Moynihan, D.W. (1994) 'Applying outcome research: intentional utilization of the client's frame of reference', *Psychotherapy* 31 (2): 294–301.

Ellingham, I. (1997) 'On the quest for a person-centred paradigm', *Counselling* 8 (1): 52–5.

Ellingham, I. (1999) 'On transcending person-centred postmodernist porridge', *Person-Centred Practice* 7 (2): 62–78.

Fairhurst, I. (1993) 'Rigid or pure?' *Person-Centred Practice* 1 (1): 25–30.

Farrell, M. (2000) 'Person-centred approach? Working with Addictions', in T. Merry (ed.), *Person-Centred Practice: The BAPCA Reader*. Ross-on-Wye: PCCS Books.

Feltham, C. (1999) 'Controversies in psychotherapy and counselling', in C. Feltham (ed.), *Controversies in Psychotherapy and Counselling*. London: Sage.

Feltham, C. (2000) 'Conceptualizing clients' problems', in C. Feltham and I. Horton (eds), *Handbook of Counselling and Psychotherapy*. London: Sage.

Feltham, C. and Horton, I. (eds) (2000) *Handbook of Counselling and Psychotherapy*. London: Sage.

Galgut, C. (1999) 'Does person-centred always equal lesbian-centred?' *Person-Centred Practice* 7 (2): 91–4.

Gaylin, N.L. (2001) *Family, Self and Psychotherapy: a Person-Centred Perspective*. Ross-on-Wye: PCCS Books.

Geller, J.D. and Gould, E. (1996) 'A contemporary psychoanalytic perspective: Rogers' brief psychotherapy with Mary Jane Tilden', in B.A. Farber, D.C. Brink and P.M. Raskin (eds), *The Psychotherapy of Carl Rogers: Cases and Commentary*. New York: Guilford Press.

Gendlin, E. (1978) *Focusing*. New York: Everest House.

Gleick, J. (1987) *Chaos: Making of a New Science*. New York: Viking Penguin.

Grant, B. (1995) 'Perfecting the therapeutic attitudes: client-centered therapy as a spiritual discipline', *The Person-Centered Journal* 2 (1): 72–7.

Hannon, J.W. (2001) 'Emancipatory person-centred counselling: postmodern theory for the 21st century', *Person-Centred Practice* 9 (1): 4–17.

Hargie, O.D.W. and Gallagher, M.S. (1992) 'A comparison of the core conditions of client-centred counselling in real and role-play counselling episodes', *Counselling* 3 (3): 153–7.

Haugh, S. (1998) 'Congruence: a confusion of language', *Person-Centred Practice* 6 (1): 44–50.

Haugh, S. and Merry, T. (eds) (2001) *Rogers' Therapeutic Conditions: Evolution, Theory and Practice. Vol. 2: Empathy*. Ross-on-Wye: PCCS Books.

Hawkins, J. (2000) 'Survivors of childhood abuse – the person-centred approach: a special contribution', in T. Merry (ed.), *Person-Centred Practice: The BAPCA Reader*. Ross-on-Wye: PCCS Books.

Hawtin, S. and Moore, J. (1998) 'Empowerment or collusion? The social context of person-centred therapy', in B. Thorne and E. Lambers (eds), *Person-Centred Therapy: a European Perspective*. London: Sage.

Hermsen, E. (1996) 'Person-centered psychology and Taoism: the reception of Lao-tzu by Carl R. Rogers', *International Journal for the Psychology of Religion* 6 (2): 107–25.

Hobbs, T. (1987). 'The Rogers interview', *Counselling Psychology Review* 4 (4): 19–27.

Holdstock, L. (1993) 'Can we afford not to revision the person-centred concept of self?' in D. Brazier (ed.) *Beyond Carl Rogers*. London: Constable.

Holdstock, L. (1990) 'Can client-centered therapy transcend its monocultural roots?', in G. Lietaer, J. Rombauts and R. van Balen (eds), *Client-Centered Experiential Psychotherapy in the Nineties*. Leuven: Leuven University Press.

Hutterer, R. (1993) 'Eclecticism: an identity crisis for person-centred therapists', in D. Brazier (ed.), *Beyond Carl Rogers*. London: Constable.

Hutterer, R., Pawlowsky, G., Schmid, P.F. and Stipsits, R. (eds) (1996) *Client-Centered and Experiential Psychotherapy: a Paradigm in Motion*. Frankfurt-am-Main: Peter Lang.

Jacobs, M. (1988) *Psychodynamic Counselling in Action*. London: Sage.

Johns, H. (1997) 'Self-development: lifelong learning?' in I. Horton and V. Sharma (eds), *The Needs of Counsellors and Psychotherapists*. London: Sage.

Jones, M. (1996) 'Person-centred theory and the post-modern turn', *Person-Centred Practice* 4 (2): 19–26.

Kalmthout, M. van (1998) 'Personality change and the concept of self', in B. Thorne and E. Lambers (eds), *Person-Centred Therapy: A European Perspective*. London: Sage.

Kearney, A. (1997) 'Class, politics and the training of counsellors', *Person-Centred Practice* 5 (2): 11–15.

Keys, S. (1999) 'The person-centred counsellor as an agent of human rights', *Person-Centred Practice* 7 (1): 41–7.

Kilborn, M. (1996) 'The quality of acceptance', *Person-Centred Practice* 4 (1): 14–23.

Kilborn, M. (1999) 'Challenge and the person-centred approach', in I. Fairhurst (ed.), *Women Writing in the Person-centred Approach*. Ross-on-Wye: PCCS Books.

Kirschenbaum, H. (1979) *On Becoming Carl Rogers*. New York: Dell.

Kirschenbaum, H. and Henderson, V.L. (eds) (1990a) *The Carl Rogers Reader*. London: Constable.

Kirschenbaum, H. and Henderson, V.L. (eds) (1990b) *The Carl Rogers Dialogues*. London: Constable.

Kovel, J. (1976) *A Complete Guide to Therapy. From Psychotherapy to Behaviour Modification*. New York: Pantheon Books.

Kuno, T. (2001) 'An interpretation of unconditional positive regard from the stand-point of Buddhist-based psychology', in J.D. Bozarth and P. Wilkins (eds), *Rogers' Therapeutic Conditions: Evolution, Theory and Practice. Vol. 3: Unconditional Positive Regard*. Ross-on-Wye: PCCS Books.

Lambers, E. (1994) 'Person-Centred psychopathology', in D. Mearns (ed.), *Developing Person-Centred Counselling*. London: Sage.

Laungani, P. (1995) 'Can psychotherapies seriously damage your health?' *Counselling* 6 (2): 110–15.

Lazarus, A.A. (1993) 'Tailoring the therapeutic relationship or being an authentic chameleon', *Psychotherapy* 30 (3): 404–7.

Leijssen, M. (1998) 'Focusing: interpersonal and intrapersonal conditions of growth', In B. Thorne and E. Lambers (eds), *Person-Centred Therapy: A European Perspective*. London: Sage.

Lietaer, G. (1984) 'Unconditional positive regard: a controversial basic attitude in client-centered therapy', in R.F. Levant and J.M. Shlien (eds), *Client-Centered Therapy and the Person-Centered Approach: New Directions in Theory, Research and Practice*. New York: Praeger.

Lietaer, G. (1993) 'Authenticity, congruence and transparency', in D. Brazier (ed.), *Beyond Carl Rogers*. London: Constable.

Lietaer, G. (1998) 'From non-directive to experiential: a paradigm unfolding', in B. Thorne and E. Lambers (eds), *Person-Centred Therapy: A European Perspective*. London: Sage.

MacMillan, M. (1999) 'In you there is a universe: person-centred counselling as a manifestation of the breath of the merciful', in I. Fairhurst (ed.), *Women Writing in the Person-Centred Approach*. Ross-on-Wye: PCCS Books.

Marshall, J. (1984) *Women Managers: Travellers in a Male World*. Chichester: Wiley.

Marshall, J. (1986) 'Exploring the experiences of women managers: towards rigour in qualitative methods', in S. Wilkinson (ed.), *Feminist Social Psychology: Developing Theory and Practice*. Milton Keynes: Open University Press.

Masson, J. (1992) *Against Therapy*. London: Fontana.

McMahon, G. (2000) 'Assessment and case formulation', in C. Feltham and I. Horton (eds), *Handbook of Counselling and Psychotherapy*. London: Sage.

McMillan, M. (1997) 'The experiencing of empathy: what is involved in achieving the "as if" condition?' *Counselling* 8 (3): 205–9.

Mearns, D. (1994) 'The dance of psychotherapy', Person-Centred Practice 2 (2): 5–13.

Mearns, D. (1996) 'Working at relational depth with clients in person-centred therapy', *Counselling* 7 (4): 306–11.

Mearns, D. (1997) *Person-Centred Counselling Training*. London: Sage.

Mearns, D. (1999) 'Person-centred therapy with configurations of self', *Counselling* 10 (2): 125–30.

Mearns, D. and McLeod, J. (1984) 'A person-centered approach to research. In R.F. Levant and J.M. Shlien (eds), *Client-Centered Therapy and the Person-Centered Approach: New Directions in Theory, Research and Practice*. New York: Praeger.

Mearns, D. and Thorne, B. (1988) *Person-Centred Counselling in Action*. London: Sage.

Mearns, D. and Thorne, B. (1999) *Person-Centred Counselling in Action* (2nd edn). London: Sage

Mearns, D. and Thorne, B. (2000) *Person-Centred Therapy Today: New Frontiers in Theory and Practice*. London: Sage.

Merry, T. (1990) 'Client-centred therapy: some trends and some troubles', *Counselling* 1 (1): 17–18.

Merry, T. (1994) Editorial, *Person-Centred Practice* 2 (1): 1–4.

Merry, T. (1995) *Invitation to Person-Centred Psychology*. London: Whurr.

Merry, T. (1996) 'An analysis of ten demonstration interviews by Carl Rogers: implications for the training of client-centred counsellors', in R. Hutterer, G. Pawlowsky, P.F. Schmid and R. Stipsits (eds), *Client-Centred and Experiential Psychotherapy: a Paradigm in Motion*. Frankfurt-am-Main: Peter Lang.

Merry, T. (1998) 'Client-centred therapy: origins and influences', *Person-Centred Practice* 6 (2): 96–103.

Merry, T. (2000) 'Person-centred counselling and therapy', in C. Feltham and I. Horton (eds), *Handbook of Counselling and Psychotherapy*. London: Sage.

Merry, T. (2001) 'Psychotherapy at the edge of awareness', *Person-Centred Practice* 9 (1): 43–8.

Mohamed, C. (2000) 'Race, culture and ethnicity', in C. Feltham and I. Horton (eds), *Handbook of Counselling and Psychotherapy*. London: Sage.

Moore, J. (2001) 'Acceptance of the truth of the present moment as a trustworthy foundation for unconditional positive regard', in J.D. Bozarth and P. Wilkins (eds), *Rogers' Therapeutic Conditions: Evolution, Theory and Practice. Vol. 3: Unconditional Positive Regard*. Ross-on-Wye: PCCS Books.

Morotomi, Y. (1998) 'Person-centred counselling from the viewpoint of Japanese spirituality', *Person-Centred Practice* 6 (1): 28–32.

Natiello, P. (1980/1999) 'Men/women issues in human development', in C. Wolter-Gustafson (ed.), *A Person-Centered Reader: A Personal Selection by Our Members*. Association for the Development of the Person Centered Approach (ADPCA).

Natiello, P. (1987) 'The person-centered approach: from theory to practice', *Person-Centered Review* 2 (2): 203–16.

Natiello, P. (1990) 'The person-centered approach, collaborative power, and cultural transformation', *Person-Centered Review* 5 (3): 268–86.

Natiello, P. (1999) 'The person-centered approach: solution to gender splitting', in I. Fairhurst (ed.), *Women Writing in the Person-Centred Approach*. Ross-on-Wye: PCCS Books.

Natiello, P. (2001) *The Person-Centred Approach: a Passionate Presence*. Ross-on-Wye: PCCS Books.

Naylor-Smith, A. (1994) 'Counselling and psychotherapy: is there a difference?' *Counselling* 5 (4): 284–6.

Neville, B. (1996) 'Five kinds of empathy', in R. Hutterer, G. Pawlowsky, P.F. Schmid and R. Stipsits (eds), *Client-Centered and Experiential Psychotherapy: a Paradigm in Motion*. Frankfurt-am-Main: Peter Lang.

O'Hara, M. (1995) 'Carl Rogers: scientist and mystic, *Journal of Humanistic Psychology* 35 (4): 40–53.

Owen, I. (1990) 'Re-emphasizing a client-centred approach', *Counselling* 1 (3): 92–4.

Owen, I.R. (1996) 'The person-centred approach in a cultural context', in S. Palmer, S. Dainow and P. Milner (eds), *Counselling: The BAC Counselling Reader*. London: Sage.

Parker, I. (1989) 'Discourse and power', in J. Shotter and K.J. Gergen (eds), *Texts of Identity*. London: Sage.

Patterson, C.H. (1984) 'Empathy, warmth, and genuineness in psychotherapy: a review of reviews', *Psychotherapy* 21 (4): 431–8.

Pilgrim, D. (2000) 'Social class', in C. Feltham and I. Horton (eds), *Handbook of Counselling and Psychotherapy*. London: Sage.

Pörtner, M. (2001) 'The person-centred approach in working with people with special needs', *Person-Centred Practice* 9 (1): 18–30.

Prouty, G.F. (1976) 'Pre-therapy, a method of treating pre-expressive psychotic and retarded patients', *Psychotherapy: Theory, Research and Practice* 13 (3): 290–5.

Prouty, G.F. (1990) 'Pre-therapy: a theoretical evolution in the person-centered/experiential psychotherapy of schizophrenia and retardation', in G. Lietaer, J. Rombauts and R. van Balen (eds), *Client-Centered and Experiential Psychotherapy in the Nineties*. Leuven: Leuven University Press.

Prouty, G.F. (1998) 'Pre-therapy and the pre-expressive self', *Person-Centred Practice* 6 (2): 80–8.

Prouty, G.F. (1999) 'Carl Rogers and experiential therapies: a dissonance?' *Person-Centred Practice* 7 (1): 4–11.

Purton, C. (1996) 'The deep structure of the core conditions: a Buddhist perspective', In R. Hutterer, G. Pawlowsky, P.F. Schmid and R. Stipsits (eds), *Client-Centered and Experiential Psychotherapy: a Paradigm in Motion*. Frankfurt-am-Main: Peter Lang.

Purton, C. (1998) 'Unconditional positive regard and its spiritual implications', in B. Thorne and E. Lambers (eds), *Person-Centred Therapy: a European Perspective*. London: Sage.

Quinn, R. (1993) 'Confronting Carl Rogers: a developmental-interactional approach to person-centered therapy', *Journal of Humanistic Psychology* 33 (1): 6–23.

Raskin, N.J. (1996) 'Person-Centred psychotherapy: twenty historical steps', in W. Dryden (ed.), *Developments in Psychotherapy: Historical Perspectives*. London: Sage.

Reason, P. and Rowan, J. (1981) *Human Inquiry: a Sourcebook of New Paradigm Research*. Chichester: Wiley.

Rennie, D.L. (1998) *Person-Centred Counselling: an Experiential Approach.* London: Sage.

Rogers, C.R. (1942) *Counseling and Psychotherapy.* Boston: Houghton Mifflin.

Rogers, C.R. (1951) *Client-Centered Therapy: Its Current Practice, Implications and Theory.* Boston: Houghton Mifflin.

Rogers, C.R. (1957) 'The necessary and sufficient conditions of therapeutic personality change', *Journal of Consulting Psychology* 21: 95–103.

Rogers, C.R. (1959) 'A theory of therapy, personality, and interpersonal relationships, as developed in the client-centered framework', in S. Koch (ed.), *Psychology: A Study of a Science, 3. Formulations of the Person and the Social Context.* New York: McGraw Hill.

Rogers, C.R. (1966) 'Client-centered therapy', in S. Arieti (ed.), *American Handbook of Psychiatry.* New York: Basic Books.

Rogers, C.R. (1967) *On Becoming a Person: a Therapist's View of Psychotherapy.* London: Constable.

Rogers, C.R. (1970) *Encounter Groups.* Harmondsworth: Penguin.

Rogers, C.R. (1975) 'Empathic: an unappreciated way of being', *The Counseling Psychologist* 5 (2): 2–11.

Rogers, C.R. (1977) *Carl Rogers on Personal Power: Inner Strength and Its Revolutionary Impact.* New York: Delacorte Press.

Rogers, C.R. (1980) *A Way of Being.* Boston: Houghton Mifflin.

Rogers, C.R. (1983) *Freedom to Learn for the 80's.* Columbus, OH: Charles E. Merrill.

Rogers, C.R. (1987) 'Comment on Shlien's article "a countertheory of transference"'. *Person-Centered Review* 2 (2): 182–8.

Rogers, N. (1985) *The Creative Connection: a Person-Centered Approach to Expressive Therapy.* Santa Rosa, CA: Person-Centered Expressive Therapy Institute.

Rowan, J. and Dryden, W. (1988) 'Innovative therapy in Britain: introduction', in J. Rowan and W. Dryden (eds), *Innovative Therapy in Britain.* Milton Keynes: Open University Press.

Sampson, E.E. (1989) 'The deconstruction of the self', In J. Shotter and K.J. Gergen (eds), *Texts of Identity.* London: Sage.

Sanders, P. (2000) 'Mapping person-centred approaches to counselling and psychotherapy', *Person-Centred Practice* 8 (2): 62–74.

Sanford, R. (1993) 'From Rogers to Gleick and back again', in D. Brazier (ed.), *Beyond Carl Rogers.* London: Constable.

Sanford, R. (1999) 'A brief history of my experience in the development of groupwork in the person-centered approach', in C. Lago and M. MacMillan (eds), *Experiences in Relatedness: Groupwork and the Person-Centred Approach.* Ross-on-Wye: PCCS Books.

Schmid, P.F. (1996) 'A person-centered approach to sexuality: intimacy, tenderness and lust', in R. Hutterer, G. Pawlowsky, P.F. Schmid and R. Stipsits (eds), *Client-Centered and Experiential Psychotherapy: a Paradigm in Motion.* Frankfurt-am-Main: Peter Lang.

Schmid, P.F. (1998) 'Face-to-face – the art of encounter', in B. Thorne and E. Lambers (eds), *Person-Centred Therapy: a European Perspective.* London: Sage.

Schmid, P.F. (2001a) 'Authenticity: the person as his or her own author. Dialogical and ethical perspectives on therapy as an encounter relationship. And beyond', in G. Wyatt (ed.), *Rogers' Therapeutic Conditions: Evolution, Theory and Practice. Vol. 1: Congruence.* Ross-on-Wye: PCCS Books.

Schmid, P.F. (2001b) 'Acknowledgement: the art of responding. Dialogical and ethical perspectives on the challenge of unconditional relationships in therapy and beyond', in J.D. Bozarth and P. Wilkins (eds), *Rogers' Therapeutic Conditions: Evolution, Theory and Practice. Vol. 3: Unconditional Positive Regard.* Ross-on-Wye: PCCS Books.

Sexton, T.L. and Whiston, S.C. (1994) 'The status of the counseling relationship: an empirical review, theoretical implications, and research directions', *The Counseling Psychologist* 22 (1): 6–78.

Shlien, J.M. (1984) 'A countertheory of transference', In R.H. Levant and J.M. Shlien (eds), *Client-Centered Therapy and the Person-Centered Approach.* New York: Praeger.

Silverstone, L. (1994) 'Person-centred art therapy: bringing the person-centred approach to the therapeutic use of art', *Person-Centred Practice* 2 (1): 18–23.

Singh, J. and Tudor, K. (1997) 'Cultural conditions of therapy', *The Person-Centered Journal* 4 (2): 32–46.

Slack, S. (1985) 'Reflections on a workshop with Carl Rogers', *Journal of Humanistic Psychology* 25 (1): 35–42.

Speierer, G.-W. (1990) 'Toward a specific illness concept of client-centered therapy', in G. Lietaer, J. Rombauts and R. van Balen (eds), *Client-Centered and Experiential Psychotherapy in the Nineties.* Leuven: Leuven University Press.

Speierer, G.-W. (1996) 'Client-centered therapy according to the Differential Incongruence Model (DIM)', in R. Hutterer, G. Pawlowsky, P.F. Schmid and R. Stipsits (eds), *Client-Centered and Experiential Psychotherapy: A Paradigm in Motion.* Frankfurt-am-Main: Peter Lang.

Spinelli, E. (1989) *The Interpreted World: An Introduction to Phenomenological Psychology.* London: Sage.

Spinelli, E. (1994) *Demystifying Therapy.* London: Constable.

Tengland, P.-A. '(2001) A conceptual exploration of incongruence and mental health', in G. Wyatt (ed.), *Rogers' Therapeutic Conditions: Evolution, Theory and Practice. Vol 1: Congruence.* Ross-on-Wye: PCCS Books.

Thorne, B. (1991) *Person-Centred Counselling: Therapeutic and Spiritual Dimensions.* London: Whurr.

Thorne, B. (1992a) *Carl Rogers.* London: Sage.

Thorne, B. (1992b) 'Psychotherapy and counselling: the quest for differences', *Counselling* 3 (4): 244–8.

Thorne, B. (1996) 'Person-centred therapy: the path to holiness', in R. Hutterer, G. Pawlowsky, P.F. Schmid and R. Stipsits (eds), *Client-Centered and Experiential Psychotherapy: a Paradigm in Motion.* Frankfurt-am-Main: Peter Lang.

Thorne, B. (2000) 'Religion and secular assumptions', in C. Feltham and I. Horton (eds), *Handbook of Counselling and Psychotherapy.* London: Sage.

Tobin, S.A. (1991) 'A comparison of psychoanalytic self psychology and Carl Rogers's person-centered therapy', *Journal of Humanistic Psychology* 31 (1): 9–33.

Tudor, K. (1997) 'The personal is political – and the political is personal: a person-centred approach to the political sphere', *Person-Centred Practice* 5 (2): 4–10.

Tudor, K. (2000) 'The case of the lost conditions', *Counselling* 11 (1): 33–7.

Tudor, K. and Merry, T. (2002) *Dictionary of Person-Centred Psychology.* London: Whurr.

Tudor, K. and Worrall, M. (1994) 'Congruence reconsidered', *British Journal of Guidance and Counselling* 22 (2): 197–205.

Warner, M.S. (1996) 'How does empathy cure? A theoretical consideration of empathy, processing and personal narrative', in R. Hutterer, G. Pawlowsky, P.F. Schmid and R. Stipsits (eds), *Client-Centered and Experiential Psychotherapy: a Paradigm in Motion.* Frankfurt-am-Main: Peter Lang.

Warner, M.S. (1998/1999) 'Person-centered psychotherapy: one nation, many tribes', in C. Wolter-Gustafson (ed.), *A Person-Centered Reader: Personal Selection by our Members.* Boston: Association for the Development of the Person-Centered Approach.

Warner, M.S. (1999) 'The language of psychology as it affects women and other traditionally disempowered groups', in I. Fairhurst (ed.), *Women Writing in the Person-Centred Approach.* Ross-on-Wye: PCCS Books.

Warner, M.S. (2000) 'Person-Centred therapy as the difficult edge: a developmentally based model of fragile and dissociated process', in D. Mearns and B. Thorne (eds), *Person-Centred Therapy Today.* London: Sage.

Waterhouse, R.L. (1993) ' "Wild women don't have the blues": a feminist critique of "person-centered" counselling and therapy', *Feminism and Psychology* 3 (1): 55–71.

Watson, J.C. and Sheckley, P. (2001) 'Potentiating growth: an examination of the research on unconditional positive regard', in J.D. Bozarth and P. Wilkins (eds), *Rogers' Therapeutic Conditions: Evolution, Theory and Practice. Vol. 3: Unconditional Positive Regard.* Ross-on-Wye: PCCS Books.

Watson, N. (1984) 'The empirical status of Rogers's hypotheses of the necessary and sufficient conditions for effective psychotherapy', in R.F. Levant and J.M. Shlien (eds), *Client-Centered Therapy and the Person-Centered Approach.* New York: Praeger.

Werde, D. van (1994) 'An Introduction to client-centred pre-therapy', in D. Mearns (ed.), *Developing Person-Centred Counselling.* London: Sage.

Wheeler, S. and McLeod, J. (1995) 'Person-centred and psychodynamic counselling: a dialogue', *Counselling* 6 (4): 283–7.

Whitmore, D. (1991) *Psychosynthesis Counselling in Action.* London: Sage.

Wilders, S. (1999) 'The person-centred approach and its relevance to substance users', in I. Fairhurst (ed.), *Women Writing in the Person-Centred Approach.* Ross-on-Wye: PCCS Books.

Wilkins, P. (1993) 'Psychodrama: a vehicle for self-integration', *Journal of the British Psychodrama Association* 8 (1): 5–17.

Wilkins, P. (1994a) 'Can psychodrama be "person-centred"? *Person-Centred Practice* 2 (2): 14–18.

Wilkins, P. (1994b) 'Sexual relationships between counsellors and ex-clients: can they ever be right?' *Counselling* 5 (3): 206–9.

Wilkins, P. (1997a) 'Empathy: a desirable quality for effective interpersonal communication?' *Applied Community Studies* 3 (2): 3–13.

Wilkins, P. (1997b) 'Congruence and countertransference: similarities and differences', *Counselling* 8 (1): 36–41.

Wilkins, P. (1997c) 'Towards a person-centred understanding of consciousness and the unconscious', *Person-Centred Practice* 5 (1): 14–20.

Wilkins, P. (1997d) 'Psychodrama and research', *British Journal of Psychodrama and Sociodrama* 12 (1 and 2): 44–61.

Wilkins, P. (1999) 'The relationship in person-centred counselling', in C. Feltham (ed.), *Understanding the Counselling Relationship.* London: Sage.

Wilkins, P. (2000a) 'Unconditional positive regard reconsidered', *British Journal of Guidance and Counselling* 28 (1): 23–36.

Wilkins, P. (2000b) 'A group's experience of process in person-centred psychodrama: a qualitative inquiry', *British Journal of Psychodrama and Sociodrama* 15 (1): 23–41.

Wilkins, P. and Bozarth, J.D. (2001) 'Unconditional positive regard in context', in J.D. Bozarth and P. Wilkins (eds), *Rogers' Therapeutic Conditions: Evolution, Theory and Practice. Vol. 3: Unconditional Positive Regard.* Ross-on-Wye: PCCS Books.

Williams, D.I. and Irving, J.A. (1996) 'Personal growth: Rogerian paradoxes', *British Journal of Guidance and Counselling* 24 (2): 165–72.

Williams, D.I. and Irving, J.A. (1997) 'Empathy', *Changes* 15 (4): 271–6.

Wolter-Gustafson, C. (1999) 'The power of the premise: reconstructing gender and human development with Rogers' theory', in I. Fairhurst (ed.), *Women Writing in the Person-Centred Approach.* Ross-on-Wye: PCCS Books.

Wood, J.K. (1996) 'The person-centered approach: towards an understanding of its implications', in R. Hutterer, G. Pawlowsky, P.F. Schmid and R. Stipsits (eds), *Client-Centered and Experiential Psychotherapy: a Paradigm in Motion.* Frankfurt-am-Main: Peter Lang.

Worsley, R. (2002) *Process Work in Person-Centred Therapy: Phenomenological and Existential Perspectives.* Basingstoke: Palgrave.

Wyatt, G. (2000) 'The multifaceted nature of congruence', *The Person-Centered Journal* 7 (1): 52–68.

Wyatt, G. (ed.) (2001) *Rogers' Therapeutic Conditions: Evolution, Theory and Practice. Vol 1: Congruence.* Ross-on-Wye: PCCS Books.

Yalom, I. (1980) *Existential Psychotherapy.* New York: Basic Books.

Zohar, D. (1990) *The Quantum Self.* London: Bloomsbury.

Index